Interpersonal Communication in the Diverse Workplace

T0311725

Foregrounding the vital importance of interpersonal communication and cultural competence in the workplace, this book offers concise, practical strategies for daily communication in a global business environment.

The workplace is steadily becoming more diverse, and cultural competence is widely recognized as a key to success, in terms of revenue, profit, market share, and workforce productivity. This and diversity appreciation are the two cornerstones for effective interpersonal communication, facilitating relationship development, improving job satisfaction, commitment, loyalty, and trust, and leading to performance and organizational success. The effectiveness of diversity training sessions and cultural guidebooks can vary – business professionals need a book that presents more than descriptions of culture-bound business practices or prescriptions for valuing diversity.

This book is that practical solution, presenting a conceptual model along with tools to put it to work from day one, including cases and examples. With its strategies for reducing diversity miscues, techniques for responding in uncomfortable conversations, and innovative ways to bridge cultural gaps, this book will help current and aspiring leaders across industries build rapport and promote constructive behaviors in a diverse work environment, resulting in organizational success.

Geraldine E. Hynes, PhD, is an award-winning, internationally experienced professional communication specialist. She offers consulting, coaching, and customized training services in presentation skills, business and professional writing, interpersonal communication, management communication, and meeting facilitation. Clients include government agencies, nonprofit organizations, and businesses in a range of sectors. She taught business communication at Sam Houston State University, Huntsville, Texas, USA, for 17 years and holds a PhD from St. Louis University.

Interpersonal Communication in the Diverse Workplace

Get Along, Get It Done, Get Ahead

Geraldine E. Hynes

Routledge
Taylor & Francis Group

NEW YORK AND LONDON

Designed cover image: © Getty//Prostock-Studio

First published 2023
by Routledge
605 Third Avenue, New York, NY 10158

and by Routledge
4 Park Square, Milton Park, Abingdon, Oxon, OX14 4RN

Routledge is an imprint of the Taylor & Francis Group, an informa business

© 2023 Geraldine E. Hynes

Library of Congress Cataloguing-in-Publication Data
Names: Hynes, Geraldine E., author.
Title: Interpersonal communication in the diverse workplace : get
along, get it done, get ahead / Geraldine E. Hynes.
Description: New York, NY : Routledge, 2023. | Includes
bibliographical references and index.
Identifiers: LCCN 2022038879 (print) | LCCN 2022038880 (ebook) |
ISBN 9781032370743 (hardback) | ISBN 9781032370736 (paperback) |
ISBN 9781003335177 (ebook)
Subjects: LCSH: Communication in management. | Business
communication. | Diversity in the workplace.
Classification: LCC HD30.3.H94 2023 (print) | LCC HD30.3 (ebook) |
DDC 658.4/5--dc23/eng/20220906
LC record available at https://lccn.loc.gov/2022038879
LC ebook record available at https://lccn.loc.gov/2022038880

ISBN: 978-1-032-37074-3 (hbk)
ISBN: 978-1-032-37073-6 (pbk)
ISBN: 978-1-003-33517-7 (ebk)

DOI: 10.4324/9781003335177

Typeset in Bembo
by MPS Limited, Dehradun

Access the Support Material: www.routledge.com/9781032370736

For

Maureen Kersting,

the epitome of this book's principles

Contents

PART IV
Get Ahead   123

Preface

I grew up on the west side of Chicago in a tough neighborhood. How tough? I remember one morning on the way to school when I spotted a dead body in a parking lot – the victim of a gangland-style shooting – surrounded by police officers. I kept walking. Mom and Dad had warned me not to talk to strangers.

As an adult, I've traveled widely and lived in several regions of the United States as well as in other countries, so I've experienced a range of cultures. For a number of years, we owned a cattle ranch in Texas. As you can imagine, life there was very different from Chicago. People were friendlier, for one thing. A woman in my fitness class once told our group that she'd lived in Texas all her life except for the three months when her husband's employer had transferred the family to another state. "I hated it there," she complained. "No one ever talked to me while we waited in line at the grocery store checkout." "Where I grew up," I thought, "we called that minding your own business."

Cultural differences often popped up in my classroom. One semester a Japanese student rose from his seat whenever I walked in. That made me feel good. Another semester my French students shook hands with me after every class. And it was common for my Texan students to hug me in greeting whenever we passed in the hallway.

The point I'm making here is that cultural diversity is a fact of life, and a lot depends on how we respond to it. We all encounter people who are different from us, and since we usually think our ways are the right ways, then their ways must be wrong. Whether it's a family member, a neighbor, or a club member, developing a relationship will be challenging because of cultural differences. Of course, you might decide you don't like them because of what they eat (or don't eat) or what they wear (or don't wear) or because of what they believe (or don't believe), and no relationship develops at all. But what about when you're at work? You might think, "Well, I have to work with them, but I don't have to like them or socialize with them." If you're a manager of a diverse workgroup, you might decide,

"I'll just treat them all alike and ignore their differences." But neither avoidance nor denial will lead to what is known as cultural competence.

The purpose of this book is to demonstrate that, first of all, diversity in the workplace is a competitive advantage, not a roadblock. Secondly, this book offers a number of practical communication strategies that will help you capitalize on the benefits of workplace diversity. Effective intercultural communication impacts both the financial and the operational performance of a business. A well-trained workforce is likely to operate successfully in a multicultural environment. However, many companies are not doing enough to overcome cultural and communication barriers. This book suggests communication behaviors that will maximize cultural competence.

The old paradigm of "managing cultural differences" has evolved beyond simple prescriptions, do's and taboos, that apply primarily when working in foreign countries. Today the goal is to develop skills and strategies that can be applied to daily interactions in any work environment. The ideas in this book will foster interpersonal relationships, which lead to increased job satisfaction, loyalty, and commitment, all of which lead to improved productivity and organizational success. By learning how to get along, you will learn how to get it done, and ultimately how to get ahead.

Acknowledgments

I am grateful to my Routledge/Taylor & Francis team for making this book a reality. Terry Clague originated the idea and convinced me it would be a valued addition to their collection. Meredith Norwich's vision was instrumental in shaping the content and structure. Bethany Nelson provided outstanding editorial assistance throughout the project. During the production stage, Radhika Bhartari, Project Manager at MPS Limited, was a patient, skillful shepherd.

Some of this book's material was drawn from my book, *Get Along, Get It Done, Get Ahead: Interpersonal Communication in the Diverse Workplace* (Business Expert Press, 2015) with the publisher's permission.

I salute Debbie DuFrene, PhD, author, editor, and Professor Emeritus of Business Communication and Legal Studies at Stephen F. Austin State University, for generously sharing her time, wisdom, and encouragement over the years, and for reviewing the manuscript.

Kevin Sanford, PhD, Professor of Business Administration at Los Angeles Valley College, also found time to review the manuscript. A true scholar and educator, he cheered me on throughout the composing process and provided thoughtful suggestions.

I am also indebted to Mike Power, Senior Instructional Designer for the College of Business Administration at Sam Houston State University, who worked his magic on the book's graphics, helping me create clear and simple illustrations of key concepts.

If you like the book cover, it's due to the expertise of Jennifer Veltsos, PhD, Professor of Technical Communication and Interim Associate Vice President at Minnesota State University, Mankato. Her visual communication skills are unparalleled.

Finally, I am most grateful to Jim Hynes, because he is always at my side and on my side.

Part I

Communication Cornerstones

Chapter 1

Diversity in the Workplace

If you're at work right now, take a look at the people around you. There's Ben, who's still a PC person, despite your repeated attempts to show him the superiority of a Mac. There's Isabelle, who irritates you because she's so closed-minded and stubborn about politics. Over there is Jose, who refuses to agree that the *Marvel Cinematic Universe* franchise is the all-time greatest blockbuster movie series.

You may not have a whole lot in common with any of the people you work with. The workplace is a loose affiliation of folks with widely different religious beliefs, political preferences, worldviews, backgrounds, and interests. Each of us is closed off from the others behind a wall built by thinking that we're right and they're just wrong. Maybe you've formed a little tribe of like-minded people with whom you can relax over lunch and review Sunday's game. If so, you probably think that work would be lots easier if only these people worked in your department.

This chapter argues that workplace diversity is not only a fact of life, it's a competitive advantage. Further, the chapter outlines strategies that you, as a manager, can adopt to capitalize on the advantages and minimize the disadvantages of workforce diversity. The trick is not to work *against* employees' differences, but to work *with* them for business success. Finally, the chapter suggests ways you can improve your communication competence when interacting with two particularly tricky populations on the job: age-diverse and gender-diverse workers.

Benefits of Workplace Diversity

If you're a tough, skeptical manager in this values-obsessed age, you've probably asked yourself, "Why can't I simply run my department in a fair, ethical way, focus on performance, treat everyone the same, and let the rest take care of itself? Why should I do anything special to 'embrace diversity'?" There are some good answers to your questions. Performance is probably the most important one. Diverse companies tend to be superior

DOI: 10.4324/9781003335177-2

performers because they realize that the best way to meet their business imperatives is to include all people as part of the talent pool.

But there are several other important reasons that managers should leverage diversity. Let's examine four that are undeniable.

Benefits of diversity:

1   Stronger customer connections
2   Innovative solutions
3   Superior performance
4   Values-driven policies

1. Stronger Connections with a Diverse Customer Base

Executives at top companies consider it obvious that being a good employer of under-represented communities will be good for marketing and customer relations in all sorts of ways. A company that has a reputation for valuing all people does have an advantage. If about 34 percent of US consumers – the total for communities of color nationwide – suspect they won't be welcome at your company, you're headed for trouble.

Successful organizations realize that when potential customers make buying decisions, they might well consider a company's reputation for cultural sensitivity. One company that recognizes the importance of meeting the needs of ever-evolving markets is Massachusetts Mutual Life Insurance (MassMutual), a 170-year-old financial services company. Their efforts to weave DEIA into company culture are not just a business strategy; they're a defining goal.

"Here at MassMutual, we know that the demographics of our nation are changing," said Sylena Echevarria, former assistant vice president of US Insurance Group, Client Services and head of the Association for Latinos at MassMutual. "As you have a more diverse consumer and customer base, your business activities, the initiatives you kick off, the products that you offer, the type of service you deliver, the interactions you have with your customers – those all need to change and evolve as well. If we don't reflect the demographics of our policy owners, we may not make the best decisions for them," Echevarria explained. "We may not understand what it is that they're looking for in order to do business with us or to retain their business."[1]

Morgan Stanley is a global financial services company with more than 55,000 employees operating in 43 countries. Like MassMutual, Morgan Stanley has formalized the effort to reach diverse markets. For example, the company supports a Multicultural Client Strategy Committee, which is tasked with focusing on the needs of clients from different backgrounds and perspectives. Simply put, when the employees on the front lines look like the customers and think like the customers, it's easier to develop trusting relationships that lead to doing more business.

2. More Innovative Solutions

Francis Bacon, a 15th-century philosopher and father of the scientific method, said, "Those who will not apply new remedies must expect new evils, for time is the greatest innovator." Companies preparing to compete in tomorrow's global economy must rely on diverse thinkers who can create innovative solutions to new problems. Diversity is a competitive advantage because different people approach similar problems in different ways. Thus, diverse groups make better decisions.

As discussed in the previous section, Morgan Stanley is a company that fosters diversity in its workforce because it strengthens relationships with its customer base. In addition, Morgan Stanley believes that diverse work-groups are better at creative problem-solving. Jeff Brodsky, former Chief Human Resources officer and Vice Chairman, said, "We believe a diverse workforce brings innovative thinking and enables us to serve our clients in a way that delivers the best financial solutions."[ii]

3. Improved Performance Effectiveness

A third benefit of workforce diversity is improved performance. Government agencies came to that realization early. One example of a federal government agency that fosters diversity to enhance performance effectiveness is the National Aeronautics and Space Administration (NASA). The team that developed Rover, the device that crawled around the surface of Mars as part of the Mars Pathfinder Mission, exhibited true diversity. The 20 people on the team included three women, one African American male, and an East Indian male, according to Donna Shirley, Head of the Mars Pathfinder Mission. In a 2000 presentation at an Innovative Thinking Conference, Shirley described the team as being diverse on other dimensions as well, including thinking style, experience, creativity, and personality. She pointed out that the diversity of talents enabled the Pathfinder project to fulfill its mission with a budget of just $264 million, roughly the same budget as for some blockbuster movies, but with better reviews.[iii]

Diversity is good for the bottom line.

Multinational corporations now agree with nonprofits and governmental agencies that diversity is linked to performance. What began for many companies as an effort to meet governmental and legal requirements has evolved into a strategic priority for success. Businesses with a committed, long-term, systematic, and strategic approach to diversity consistently show better performance.[iv]

Ford Motor Company is an example of a corporation that has created metrics to prove the impact of diversity initiatives on the company's overall business strategy. At Ford, for instance, employee resource groups (ERGs) demonstrate their value to the bottom line by tracking the number of vehicles members sell through the company's Friends and Neighbors vehicle discount plan. According to Michele Jayne, former Global People Strategy Lead now retired from Ford, "Achieving a diverse workforce and effectively managing this workforce can yield huge benefits."[v] Simply put, diversity is good for the bottom line.

4. The Right Thing to Do

Superior performance may be the most practical reason to welcome diversity, but occasionally the moral argument is heard – making a company especially friendly to culturally diverse groups is worth doing simply because it's the right and ethical thing to do. Organizations have a duty to act as corporate citizens, regardless of the economic implications. Tony Burns, former CEO of Ryder Trucks and onetime president of the Urban League, believed that his company's efforts toward minorities were good business, but he also said that he launched initiatives to diversify his employee base without knowing for sure that it would pay off. So why did he launch them? "Because it was the right thing to do."[vi]

Today's organizations are held to a standard of consistency between their stated values and their actual policies. When a company's mission and vision statement includes a clause about diversity, then they are expected to walk the talk. Empty gestures toward inclusiveness are quickly exposed, and reputations suffer.

To summarize, it's a safe bet to predict that companies will continue to foster diversity among their workforce and business partners, for at least four reasons: stronger customer connections, innovative solutions to business problems, superior performance, and the moral imperative. The next section of this chapter focuses on concrete actions that organizations are taking to foster diversity. Hopefully, you will find some good ideas to take back to work.

Organizational Strategies for Welcoming and Supporting Diversity

There are no secrets to successful recruiting, supporting, and leveraging diversity in business environments. Companies with enviable track records have implemented a range of strategies that you and your organization might also be able to adopt. The days are long gone when inclusiveness meant merely serving fajitas in the company cafeteria on Cinco de Mayo (a national holiday in Mexico commemorating their victory over French forces at the Battle of Puebla on May 5, 1862). The following paragraphs describe five strategies for welcoming diversity and explain how they apply in certain companies.

Ways to support diversity:

1   Recruit diverse employees
2   Ensure diversity at leadership levels
3   Establish employee support groups
4   Establish mentorship programs
5   Partner with diverse companies

1. Recruit Diverse Employees

As described earlier in this chapter, Massachusetts Mutual Life Insurance Company and Morgan Stanley are companies committed to diversity. They strive to reach out to community partners and to recruit and retain workforces that incorporate a range of cultures, backgrounds, experiences, and perspectives. Both businesses actively recruit talent from historically underrepresented backgrounds and communities. Recruiters search for potential employees as early as high school. They partner with prestigious universities, campus diversity groups, and other organizations committed to diversity such as the National Association of Black Accountants.

2. Ensure Diversity at the Top Levels

The leadership of truly diverse organizations will also reflect diversity. MassMutual's efforts to diversify the workforce extend to the very top. Women and people of color compose nearly half of all seats on the board of directors.[vii] The company's Diversity Recruitment Strategy engages Asian, Hispanic, Latino, African-American women, and LGBTQ+ partners as decision-makers in crafting initiatives to recruit, retain, develop, and cultivate future leaders.

Prudential, another financial services multinational company, is led by a diverse board of directors. It is composed of four directors who have worked outside the United States, two directors who are African-American, one director who is Asian–American, and two who are Hispanic; four of the thirteen directors are women and one director is LGBTQ+. Furthermore, women compose nearly 40 percent of Prudential's leaders.[viii]

The National Football League represents another kind of business that uses an aggressive approach to ensuring diversity at the leadership level. For example, Jonathan Beane, the NFL's Chief Diversity and Inclusion Officer, had identified a need for top-level candidates to reach decision-makers. So in 2022, the League hosted a Coach and Front Office Accelerator. The Accelerator convened more than 60 diverse head coaches and GM prospects with representatives from all 32 clubs. The program provided leadership development sessions as well as time spent networking directly with club owners. "This program is the latest in a series of steps designed to improve our hiring practices and create opportunities for advancement," said NFL Commissioner Roger Goodell.[ix] Beane reiterated the NFL's goals: "I hope the owners walk away … with a clear understanding on a broad level of why it is so important to ensure that our head coaches, our GMs and the rest of the senior roles we have at the National Football League are representative of society at large and our fan base."[x]

3. Establish Employee Networking Groups

To provide channels that will carry a diversity of ideas and thought upward, MassMutual established a Women's Leadership Network and eight business resource groups (BRGs), support groups for specific employee populations. Under-represented groups sometimes believe that the best way to advance is to work hard and blend in, but BRGs take a different approach, allowing them to leverage their backgrounds, speak their minds, and share ideas. More than 30 percent of MassMutual's employees participate in BRGs, which represent Black/African American, Asian, and Hispanic/Latino/Latinx communities, members of the LGBTQ+ community, individuals with disabilities and their caregivers, armed forces members, veterans and military family members, young professionals, and women leaders. In 2021, the BRGs organized quarterly events to raise employees' cultural competence, reaching nearly 3,000 employees.[xi]

Another example of a company-supported employee networking group is Morgan Stanley's work-life integration program. This group addresses working parent and family concerns as well as the need for increased flexibility. Other employee networking groups provide opportunities for workers to celebrate their cultures and support local organizations while increasing positive exposure and relationship building.

Prudential is a third example of a company that creates and supports employee networks charged with promoting social activities and professional development. Among the groups is "VetNet," for active members of the military, veterans, and veterans' partners. Another is the EAGLES

(Employee Association of Gay Men, Lesbians, Bisexuals, Transgenders, and Allies), a group that helped conduct research on the financial and legal concerns of same-sex couples and LGBTQ+ parents.

4. Establish Mentorship Programs

As support groups for employees of similar backgrounds, MassMutual's BRGs provide mentors and leadership programs. Sylena Echevarria, former assistant vice president of US Insurance Group, Client Services, says, "I never thought I'd be in the position I am today because there weren't people around me when I was growing up who worked in a professional setting that I could look to share experiences."[xii]

Erica Bowman is a first-generation daughter of a Korean immigrant and was also the first in her family to go to college. After working in the financial services industry for several years, she took a break from her career to start a family. When ready to return to the workforce, she was attracted to Morgan Stanley's mentoring program, "Return to Work," a 12-week paid internship that pairs participants with senior-level leaders. Bowman says, "The fact that we had this breadth of support during the program made a huge difference in acclimating to the job and the firm as a whole." Today, Bowman is a Vice President in Investment Management and COO of Global Marketing for Morgan Stanley.[xiii]

MasterCard is another corporation that provides mentoring as a way to help employees connect with co-workers across the business who have similar ambitions and interests. The company pairs mentors and mentees based on capabilities and ambitions, instead of making matches based solely on seniority. As their Chief Talent and Organizational Effectiveness Officer, Lucrecia Borgonovo, notes, "We've been trying to demystify mentoring through our opportunity marketplace. We're telling people that mentoring isn't just about career advancement, we're trying to position mentoring as more skill-based and domain knowledge-based."[xiv]

5. Seek Diversity among Business Partners

The diversity benefits identified in this chapter certainly operate in business-to-business and even business-to-government partnerships. Prudential is one example of a company that actively seeks out vendors and business partners from broad backgrounds and varying perspectives. Their stated goal is to do business with vendors that reflect the demographics of local markets. Prudential actively seeks bids and proposals from business enterprises that are owned by minorities, women, veterans, service-disabled veterans, representatives of the LGBTQ+ community, and people with disabilities.

Genentech, an American biotechnology corporation, also knows that DEIA values are critical to their success. Embracing DEIA beyond their walls improves scientific and clinical outcomes and helps contribute to equitable healthcare access around the globe. As part of their efforts, Genentech invests in partnerships that strengthen DEIA across the healthcare profession. "Our mission is to deliver scientific innovations that drive better outcomes for our people, patients, business, and communities by advancing and boldly championing diversity, equity, and inclusion," says Quita Beeler Highsmith, Chief Diversity Officer.[xv]

Communicating with Diverse Workers

Once you've recognized that workplace diversity contributes important advantages to an organization and you've identified ways that your organization can welcome and support a pluralistic work environment, you may be wondering how diversity affects your own daily communication patterns. After all, the purpose of this book is to help you improve your managerial communication skills.

Diversity sensitivity leads to effective managerial communication.

If your communication behavior reflects your sensitivity to differences, it will be more successful and effective. This section describes how two very common types of workplace diversity – age and gender – influence managers' interaction styles and how you can improve your ability to communicate with each population.

Age Diversity

Americans are living longer, and the average employee is getting older. For the first time ever, four generations are working together. Every generation is different, and generation gaps are natural. If you are in your 20s or 30s, you may well find yourself managing people old enough to be your parents or even your grandparents. How awkward is that?

What do older workers fear? Let's step into their shoes for a minute and make a list:

- New technology
- Younger employees
- Discrimination
- Obsolescence
- Changes in the workplace

Older workers are likely to feel dominant, perhaps because of their years of experience. Many are still vigorous, healthy, intellectually curious, and unwilling to retire. They seek stimulation and opportunities to continue contributing to society.

Are there any values differences or attitudinal differences between older workers and younger managers? Yes, there appear to be several that are relevant to workplace relationships.

Generational differences in values:

- Attitudes toward authority
- Importance of seniority
- Attitudes toward organizations and groups

- *Attitudes toward authority* – Boomers came of age in the 1960s, when challenging authority was a rite of passage. They marched for social justice and sat in for peace. Although most people in their generation eventually became part of, or even leaders of, The Establishment, rebellion is still considered an option.
- *Importance of seniority* – Boomers expect respect because they've come so far and cast such a long shadow all their lives. Surviving, whether it's the Vietnam War, 9/11, or the Covid pandemic, counts. They honor rank, chain of command, and organizational hierarchies, including job titles. Office artifacts that symbolize achievements such as trophies, certificates, and plaques, are displayed with pride.
- *Attitudes toward organizations and groups* – Boomers are joiners. Membership in professional associations and workgroups is valued, and they wear their Rotary Club lapel pins with pride. They show up for high school reunions; younger generations don't have to go to reunions because they stay in touch with classmates on social media. They believe in teamwork.

If you manage older employees, here are some communication tips:

- Get at the roots of the problem rather than working from assumptions
- Be specific about inappropriate behaviors; don't generalize or stereotype
- Encourage the employees to vent and express themselves
- Demonstrate empathy and respect

Managing older workers with performance problems may require that you seek more creative solutions. Think of ways to capitalize on their life experience by offering mentoring opportunities and special assignments. To help keep their skills up to date, provide more job sharing, job rotation, and training. Working in teams with younger peers will allow each generation to recognize the other's strengths and better understand their worldviews.

Strategies for managing older workers:

- Mentoring opportunities
- Special assignments
- Job sharing
- Short-term projects
- Job rotation
- Training
- Heterogeneous teams

Now let's look at the reverse situation – older managers in charge of younger generations of workers. Generational tensions seem especially strong between managers born from 1965 to 1980 (called Generation X) and direct reports born from 1980 to 1994 (Millennials). According to Harvard Business School researchers, Gen Xers started working when the economy was slow, and their career paths were rocky. Feeling vulnerable, they made personal and family sacrifices to achieve success. Today, the Millennial employees they manage are less willing to sacrifice their time with their families. They expect to be evaluated for productivity, not hours at their desk, especially because they are tech-savvy, which makes their geographic location irrelevant. Their loyalties lie with their social network rather than their job, and they do not fear change.[xvi]

Strategies for managing younger workers:

- Flextime
- Focus on goals, not methods
- Technology tools
- Variety
- Long-term projects
- Heterogeneous teams

By 2020, fully half of the US workforce was made up of Millennials. Their values and attitudes have influenced the workplace in interesting ways. For instance, new corporate office buildings are designed for maximum natural light, with high ceilings, outdoor areas, and common spaces rather than small offices and cubicles. The emphasis is on "we" space rather than "me" space.[xvii] Companies such as ExxonMobil and Anadarko currently provide amenities such as fitness centers, jogging trails, bicycle racks, and wellness centers to attract and keep younger employees. During the Covid-19 pandemic, Millennials flourished at the opportunity to work from home, proving that productivity and working relationships are not strongly related to physical proximity.

As Generation Z, born from 1995 to 2012, enters the workplace, we see some differences from Millennial employees. While Millennials value teamwork, Gen Z workers appear to be more entrepreneurial, independent, and competitive. They also are less motivated by financial success than Millennials.

On the other hand, there are striking similarities between Gen Zs and Millennials in terms of their workplace attitudes and behaviors. For one thing, both generations are digital natives, perfectly comfortable working with technology. Another similarity is that DEIA is a top priority for both these groups, so leading by example is key to managing and retaining them as employees. Third, both generations expect to change jobs every few years, which implies limits to employer loyalty. LinkedIn CEO Ryan Roslansky found that job transitions on LinkedIn increased by 80 percent for Gen Z and 50 percent for Millennials in 2021.[xviii] Paving the way for post-pandemic work environments, Millennials and Gen Z employees expect workplace autonomy, flexibility, and an emphasis on well-being. The COVID-19 pandemic seems to have dramatically affected their outlook; many agree that "life is short," which means they are less likely to stay in unfulfilling jobs. Thus, a key to retaining younger workers is respecting differences.

One step toward developing sensitivity for age-related differences is to monitor your language regarding status in the workplace. Whether you are significantly older or younger than your employees, try to avoid terms that unnecessarily emphasize hierarchical rank. Instead, when referring to your work group, use terms that emphasize roles, spans of responsibility, and equity. Table 1.1 offers equitable language options.

Clearly, when diverse employees' values clash, effective communication across the generational divide becomes even more important. An effective manager is sensitive to age diversity because of its implications for employee retention, harmony, efficiency, and productivity.

Table 1.1 Terms for Employees

Status Emphasis	Roles Emphasis	Equity Emphasis
Superior	Staff	Associate
Subordinate	Direct Report	Colleague
Leader	Worker	Coworker
Follower	Contributor	Team member
	Assistant	Stakeholder
	Contact person	Constituent

Gender Diversity

Over the past 30 years, researchers have closely examined masculine and feminine communication styles at work, but results have been inconsistent because of the complexity of contributing factors. Social scientist Deborah Tannen found strong evidence for gender differences in communication styles. In doing so, she also presented interesting reasons men and women have difficulty communicating with each other. These reasons include both innate traits and learned behavior.[xix] Some of the gender differences in workplace conversations that Tannen identified are shown in Table 1.2, along with example statements.

Researchers have identified differences in listening styles as well as speaking styles. For instance, feminine communicators may be more likely to listen to affirm both the relationship and the person who is speaking, zooming in on an emotional level and being empathic, while masculine

Table 1.2 Masculine and Feminine Communication Styles

Masculine	Example	Feminine	Example
Asks for information	Who's the expert on this software?	Asks for help	I need help learning this software.
Uses report-talk	These are the facts.	Uses rapport-talk	We're happy with this solution.
Uses powerful language	That won't work.	Uses powerless language	I may be wrong, so stop me if you disagree, but I think there may be roadblocks.
Complains	By missing the deadline you wrecked my project's schedule.	Apologizes	I'm sorry to hear that you can't meet the deadline.

communicators often tend to listen for the facts and information in a message and may be less comfortable handling its emotional content. They may be more likely to listen for solutions and more willing to give advice than empathy.[xx]

Such differences in communication style among genders don't appear to be diminishing; in fact, gender diversity of the workforce is increasing, as is the importance of respecting how someone self-identifies. As a manager, you can indicate your understanding that the world is currently gender expansive, including more than just two options, by adapting your language to signal inclusiveness. One habit is to use their chosen pronouns. How will you know everyone's appropriate pronouns? The simplest approach is to ask people what words they use to describe themselves. Some workers include their pronouns in their email signatures.

Managers can indicate respect for their employees by using inclusive language.

Similarly, you can indicate sensitivity to gender diversity when communicating by using gender-neutral pronouns to stand for any person. Try replacing gender-specific pronouns (he, she, her, him) with the gender-neutral version (they, them). Yes, "they" and "them" once stood for plural nouns (people, workers) rather than singular ones (person, worker), but grammar rules change over time.

If you're getting confused, Table 1.3 will refresh your knowledge of pronoun usage. The Table shows that, in English, pronouns referring to people have two characteristics: person (first, second, third) and number (singular, plural). The cell for third person singular pronouns is the only cell in the Table that has gender-specific pronouns. If a speaker uses these pronouns, they risk making a wrong assumption. The easy solution is to avoid gender-indicating pronouns either by using the singular "they," as suggested in the preceding paragraph, or the second person pronoun, "you." Not only is "you" gender-neutral, it has

Table 1.3 Gender-Specific and Gender-Neutral Pronouns

Person	Singular	Plural
First	I, me	We, us
Second	You	You
Third	He, she, him, her, they, them	They, them

added benefits – "you" can stand for one person or more than one, plus it's more engaging because it directly addresses the audience.

A second way to indicate sensitivity to gender diversity when communicating is your use of courtesy titles. Once upon a time, it was customary to precede names with Mr., Mrs., Ms., Sir, Madam, or Miss, all of which are gender-specific, binary terms. Today, most professional communication has dropped courtesy titles, but if your organization's writing style still includes them, consider the gender-neutral Mx instead.

A third way to indicate sensitivity to gender diversity when you are addressing a work group is to avoid slang terms like "you guys" or similar terms that assume their gender. Some people may react negatively to being addressed as "girls," "gals," "ladies," "guys," or "fellas." The US Bureau of Labor Statistics estimated that women would be the majority of the workforce by 2022.[xxi] And women have rapidly moved into management. Indeed, the number of women serving as corporate officers in the top ten Fortune 500 companies doubled in the past 20 years.[xxii] Abigail Johnson, president and CEO of Fidelity Investments, was ranked the sixth most powerful woman in the world by Forbes in 2021. She understands that diverse workforces require tactful styles of communication. "I had to learn to communicate to very different types of groups of managers with different orientations, different priorities," she recalls.[xxiii] The payoff is that companies with more gender diversity have more revenue, customers, market share, and profits.[xxiv]

In short, effective managers are conscious of cultural differences and make special efforts to use inclusive language. You're better off considering differences in characteristics like gender and age to be complementary rather than problematic, since research shows that diversity in work teams leads to better outcomes. In addition to making these language adjustments when you are speaking and writing, encourage your employees to use gender-neutral pronouns, eliminate or adjust courtesy titles, and avoid gender-specific slang terms when communicating. Remember that innovation, creativity, and intelligence are age-free, culture-free, and gender-free.[xxv] Everyone will be more likely to achieve their organization's goals if they form habits of respectful, courteous, inclusive language.

Summary

The first cornerstone of communication competence in today's diverse workplace is recognition of its benefits. Major benefits of a diverse workforce include stronger customer connections, more innovative solutions, superior performance, and values-driven policies. Top organizations apply a number of strategies for welcoming and supporting diversity such as recruiting diverse employees, promoting diversity at leadership levels, establishing employee support groups, establishing mentorship programs, and partnering with diverse companies.

Two types of diversity are particularly important for today's managers: age and gender. Relevant values and mindsets that differ across generations include attitudes toward authority, the importance of seniority, and attitudes toward organizations. Major differences in communication style among genders appear to be persistent, and they are important because of the increasing gender diversity of the workforce. Effective managerial communication is sensitive to differences in characteristics including gender and age, since research shows that diversity in work teams leads to better outcomes.

Notes

i "Leadership in Diversity and Inclusion," (2014, November 9). *New York Times Magazine,* pp. 54–58.

ii "Leadership in Diversity and Inclusion," p. 56.

iii Donna Shirley (2000, March 7). Presentation at Innovative Thinking Conference, Scottsdale, Arizona. See also Donna Shirley (1998). *Managing Martians: The Extraordinary Story of a Woman's Lifelong Quest to Get to Mars – and of the Team behind the Space Robot That Captured the Imagination of the World* (New York: Broadway Books).

iv Kochan, T., Bezrukova, K., Ely, R., Jackson, S., Joshi, A., Jehn, K., et al. (2003). "The Effects of Diversity on Business Performance: Report of the Diversity Research Network." *Human Resource Management,* Vol. 42, pp. 3–21.

v Michele E.A. Jayne and Robert Dipboye (2004, Winter). "Leveraging Diversity to Improve Business Performance: Research Findings and Recommendations for Organizations." *Human Resource Management,* Vol. 43, no. 4, pp. 409–424.

vi Geoffrey Colvin (1999, July 19). "Outperforming the S&P 500: Companies that Pursue Diversity Outperform the S&P 500. Coincidence?" *Fortune,* Vol. 140, no. 2, pp. 52–58.

vii MassMutual, "Our Commitment to Diversity, Equity, and Inclusion" (2021). Retrieved from https://www.massmutual.com/sustainability/diversity-equity-and-inclusion/unity-messaging

viii Prudential Financial, Inc. Proxy Statement (2022). Retrieved from https://www.prudential.com/links/about/board-of-directors

ix "Inaugural NFL Coach and Front Office Accelerator Program" (2022, May 19). Retrieved from https://www.nfl.com/news/inaugural-nfl-coach-and-front-office-accelerator-program-slated-for-spring-league

x Albert Breer (2022, May 19). "Inside the Plans for the NFL's First Diversity Networking Event," *Sports Illustrated.* Retrieved from https://www.si.com/nfl/2022/05/19/nfl-diversity-networking-event-plans-spring-meeting

xi MassMutual Sustainability Report (2021), p. 18. Retrieved from https://www.massmutual.com/global/media/shared/doc/sustainability/2021sustainabilityreport.pdf#page=23

xii "Leadership in Diversity and Inclusion," p. 57.

xiii Morgan Stanley, "A Single Mom Returns to Work" (2021, November 8). Retrieved from https://www.morganstanley.com/articles/return-to-work-single-mom-erica-bowman

xiv Nicole Schreiber-Shearer (2022, April 11). "3 Companies Showcasing Successful Mentorship Programs," Retrieved from https://gloat.com/blog/successful-mentorship-programs/

xv   Dominique Fluker (2021, May 8). "12 Companies Ramping Up Their Diversity & Inclusion Efforts – and How You Can Too," *Glassdoor for Employers*. Retrieved from https://www.glassdoor.com/employers/blog/inspiration-for-ramping-up-diversity-inclusion-efforts/

xvi   Skye Schooley (2022, July 7). "How to Be a Good Manager," *Business News Daily*. Retrieved from https://www.businessnewsdaily.com/6129-good-manager-skills.html

xvii   Nancy Sarnoff (2014, June 13). "Younger Workers Crave 'Sense of Place' on the Job." *Houston Chronicle*, p. D1.

xviii   Hillary Hoffower (2022, May 8). "Meet the Typical Gen Z Worker, Who Is Quitting Their Job for a Better One but Probably Regretting It Later," *Business Insider*. Retrieved from https://www.businessinsider.com/what-gen-z-wants-workplace-expecations-salary-benefits-perks-2022-5

xix   Deborah Tannen (2007). *You Just Don't Understand: Women and Men in Conversation* (New York: William Morrow).

xx   Julia T. Wood (2013). *Gendered Lives: Communication, Gender, and Culture*, 10th Ed. (Boston: Wadsworth), p. 127.

xxi   Mitra Toossi, "Labor Force Projections to 2022," *Monthly Labor Review*, December 2013. Retrieved from www.bls.gov/EMP.

xxii   Sallie Krawcheck, "Diversify Corporate America," *Time*, March 24, 2014, pp. 36–37.

xxiii   Moira Forbes (2013, November 1). "7 Career Lessons from Billionaire Abigail Johnson," *Forbes*. Retrieved from https://www.forbes.com/sites/moiraforbes/2013/11/01/seven-career-lessons-from-billionaire-abigail-johnson/?sh=26d83d8276a1

xxiv   Adam Grant and Sheryl Sandberg (2014, December 7). "Women at Work: When Talking about Bias Backfires." *The New York Times*, p. 3SR.

xxv   Maureen Taylor (2022, March 14). "How to Communicate Well with People from Other Cultures." *wikiHow* blog. Retrieved from https://www.wikihow.com/Communicate-Well-With-People-from-Other-Cultures

Chapter 2

Cultural Competence

Part I lays two "cornerstones" or basic concepts that are the foundation on which the framework of this book is built. The first cornerstone is *diversity appreciation*. In Chapter 1 we discussed the increasing diversity of the workforce and considered four competitive advantages that diversity offers. We also examined communication strategies that you, as a manager, can adopt to capitalize on the advantages of workforce diversity.

This chapter describes our second cornerstone, *cultural competence* (Figure 2.1). Diversity brings with it different cultural norms, leadership styles, and communication patterns, so you can see the critical link between cultural competence and your success as a manager. If you know how to navigate among cultural differences, you will be equipped to develop positive relationships with your employees, relationships that lead to productivity, profits, and organizational success.

What is Cultural Competence?

Corporate response to the increasing diversity of the workforce varies widely, but cultural competence is generally valued. Cultural competence is defined as being "comfortable working with colleagues and customers from diverse cultural backgrounds."[i] Cultural competence can be considered an outgrowth of the DEIA (diversity, equity, inclusion, and accessibility) principles described in Chapter 1. Indeed, today's employers consider intercultural communication skills as a key factor when hiring. In 2020, Leadership IQ surveyed over 1,400 hiring managers in a range of industries and company sizes to determine the factors affecting their new hires' failure rate. Results of the survey indicate that technical skills are not the primary reason why new hires fail; instead, poor interpersonal skills dominate the list, such as coachability, motivation, emotional intelligence, and temperament that fits their corporate culture. Based on these findings, Mark Murphy, Leadership IQ's CEO, advises companies that embrace DEIA principles to carefully assess job candidates' cultural competence during the hiring process.[ii]

DOI: 10.4324/9781003335177-3

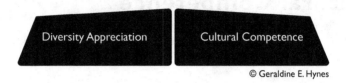

© Geraldine E. Hynes

Figure 2.1 Cornerstones of the Sequence for Success.

Reactions to diversity in business:

1   Affirmative action
2   Inclusion
3   Cultural competence

Briefly, a culturally competent manager understands that culture profoundly affects workplace behavior and attitudes. Furthermore, a culturally competent manager knows how to navigate relevant cultural differences in order to maximize workers' loyalty, satisfaction, productivity, and ultimately the bottom line. *The Economist* Intelligence Unit surveyed 572 executives in multinational organizations and found that they overwhelmingly agreed that cultural competence improves revenues (89 percent), profits (89 percent), and market share (85 percent). The executives also widely agreed that managerial communication skills are essential for workforce productivity.[iii]

Why Culture Matters

Let's take a closer look at the notion of culture so we can see why it's such an important factor in managerial success. Culture is what we grow up in. Beginning in childhood, we learn acceptable behaviors, customs, and habits. We also adopt the beliefs, values, and moral attitudes of the society in which we mature. A body of common understanding develops. We know what to expect, and we know what is expected of us.[iv]

Culture is what we grow up in.

Defined in such a way, culture includes the religious systems to which we are exposed, the educational system, the economic system, the political system, the legal system, morals, recreational outlets, mores governing dress and grooming, standards of etiquette, food and how it is prepared and served, gift-giving customs, quality and quantity of communication among people, greeting practices, rituals, modes of travel available, as well as the many other aspects of our lives.

There is some evidence that culture can even affect our personalities. For instance, a series of studies of people who spoke both Spanish and English showed that switching languages significantly affected personality variables such as extraversion (or assertiveness), agreeableness (superficial friendliness), and conscientiousness (achievement).[v] Multilingualism is becoming more common in the United States, especially among the younger generation. According to the US Census Bureau, Millennials are the most diverse generation in history, with one in four speaking a non-English language at home.

Furthermore, culture can influence the way we see the world. If you show pictures of a monkey, a panda, and a banana to someone from Japan and ask which two go together, chances are that the Japanese will pick the monkey and the banana, because the former eats the latter. Show the same pictures to someone from Great Britain and she is more likely to select the panda and the monkey, because they are both mammals. Westerners typically see classifications where Asians see relationships.

There is strong evidence that these differences in worldviews begin from birth. In another study, Japanese and American children were asked to look at a tank of large fish, small fish, and some aquarium plants and rocks. When they were asked what they saw, the Japanese kids described the groups of fish and the environmental elements. The American kids talked about the big fish.[vi] The researchers concluded that the collectivist Japanese culture encourages youngsters to focus on groups, while the individualist US kids learn early on to focus on standouts.

Malcolm Gladwell explored the importance of culture in his best-seller, *Outliers: The Story of Success*. He concluded, "Cultural legacies are powerful forces. They have deep roots and long lives. They persist, generation after generation, virtually intact ... and we cannot make sense of our world without them."[vii]

A Closer Look at Cultural Differences

What are the "deep roots" of cultural differences that Gladwell was referring to? One of the most extensive studies of cultural differences was conducted at IBM Corporation by a Dutch management thinker, Geert Hofstede. He surveyed more than 116,000 IBM employees in 40 countries. A massive statistical analysis of his findings revealed six dimensions of national culture as shown in Figure 2.2: power distance, uncertainty

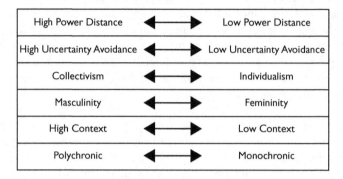

Figure 2.2 Hofstede's Dimensions of Cultural Differences.

avoidance, individualism/collectivism, masculinity/femininity, high and low context, and monochronic/polychronic time.[viii] Examining Hofstede's framework can help you anticipate and then solve possible problems caused by misunderstandings between employees from different cultures.

Power distance indicates the extent to which a society accepts the fact that power is distributed unequally, according to Hofstede's theory. It is reflected in the values of both the more powerful and less powerful members of society. The Philippines, Venezuela, and Mexico are countries with high power distances; and Denmark, New Zealand, the United States, and Israel are a few of the countries with low power distances.[ix]

> **High/Low Power Distance: the extent to which society accepts the unequal distribution of power.**

A manager in a culture with high power distance is seen as having dramatically more power than a direct report would have. This manager, who usually is addressed respectfully by title and surname, might favor a controlling strategy and behave like an autocrat. For instance, within the British Houses of Parliament, lawmakers can move to the head of the line at restaurants, restrooms, and elevators, while clerks, aides, and secretaries who work in Parliament must stand and wait. In a culture with a lower power distance, on the other hand, managers are seen as having little more power than their direct reports, are typically addressed by their given name, take a place in line, and communicate with equalitarian strategies.

Uncertainty avoidance relates to the degree to which a society feels threatened by uncertainty and by ambiguous situations, according to Hofstede. People within such a society try to avoid these uncertainties and ambiguous situations by providing greater career stability, establishing and following formal rules, discouraging odd ideas and behaviors, and believing in absolute truths and the attainment of expertise. Greece, Germany, England, and Japan have strong uncertainty avoidance, while Hong Kong, Denmark, the United States, and Sweden have weak uncertainty avoidance.[x]

High/Low Uncertainty Avoidance: the extent to which society feels threatened by ambiguity.

If you are managing employees whose culture values uncertainty avoidance, you will have difficulty getting them to embrace change, since they will likely prefer the status quo. To reduce resistance, try to get them involved in the new strategy and highlight the benefits of change.

On Hofstede's *individualism/collectivism* dimension, *individualism* suggests a loosely knit social framework in which people are expected to take care of themselves and their immediate families only. *Collectivism,* by contrast, is a tight social framework in which people distinguish between in-groups and out-groups. They expect their group (relatives, clan, organization) to take care of them; and because of that, they believe they owe absolute loyalty to their group. The United States, Australia, and Great Britain are highly individualistic countries on Hofstede's scale, while Pakistan, Colombia, Nigeria, and Venezuela are more collectivist countries.[xi]

Individualism/Collectivism: the extent to which society prefers loyalty to the group over loyalty to the individual.

If you are a manager from an individualistic culture and you are participating in negotiations with business professionals from a collectivist culture, you may be frustrated when you push them toward making quick decisions. They must first collaborate to reach consensus. You might ask to talk to a "decision maker," but there probably won't be one. Be patient while the other group spends time in conference.

Masculinity/femininity is the fourth Hofstede dimension. According to this theory, masculinity includes assertiveness, the acquisition of money and things, and not caring about the quality of life. These values are labeled masculine because, within nearly all societies, men scored higher in these values than women. Japan, Austria, and Mexico scored among the most masculine societies. Feminine cultures, by contrast, value family, children, and quality of life. Denmark, Sweden, and Norway are considered feminine cultures.[xii]

> Masculinity/Femininity: the extent to which society values quality of life.

Consider the following example. In the United States people are judged at least partly on their ability to make a good salary. Frequently, this judgment precludes traditional US feminine values of caring for children. Despite the passage of the Family Leave Act in 1993, the majority of US working men and women do not take the full amount of time they are eligible for when dealing with family and medical problems.

Context is the fifth cultural difference in Hofstede's model. In a *high-context* culture, much information is gathered from the physical context or environment or the person's behavior. People look for meaning in what is not said – in the nonverbal communication or body language; in the silences, the facial expressions, and the gestures. Japan and Saudi Arabia are high-context countries, as are Chinese- and Spanish-speaking countries, according to Hofstede's research.[xiii]

> High/Low Context: the extent to which society gathers information from the environment.

In a *low-context* culture, most information comes from the language. In such a culture, communicators emphasize sending and receiving accurate messages directly, usually by being highly articulate. Canada and the United States are low-context cultures. As you might suspect, negotiations between low-context and high-context cultures can be tricky. The value of contracts and documents used in business-to-business transactions will vary by culture. In high-context countries, agreements are sealed with simple handshakes between those with strong personal relationships.

The sixth dimension of cultural differences, according to Hofstede, is *monochronic vs. polychronic* time. In a monochronic culture, such as Germany, the United States, and most westernized nations, we frequently talk about saving time, wasting time, making time, and spending time. We measure time by the clock, often in nanoseconds. In hyper-punctual countries like

Japan, pedestrians walk fast and bank clocks are accurate. In Western businesses we read quarterly returns and define "long-term" projections as those going out three to five years into the future. Time is linear in that Westerners believe we move forward in a linear fashion as the universe ages.[xiv]

Monochronic/Polychronic: the way a society perceives time.

By contrast, in polychronic cultures such as Spain, Latin America, and most Asian countries, time just *is*. These cultures trace their roots back thousands of years. Time is measured by events, not the clock. Everything moves in a circular path. Thus, promptness diminishes in value, although being "late" is often a sign of status in a polychronic culture.[xv] People are generally more patient, less interested in time management or measurement, and more willing to wait for their rewards than those in monochronic cultures. A culturally competent manager will recognize that differences among employees, customers, and other stakeholders regarding the perception of time may well be culture-bound. Accepting, even valuing, such differences is critical for global business success.

Developing Cultural Competence

All of us can benefit from increasing our understanding of cultural differences. Now that we have explored the deep roots of some of these differences, as described in Hofstede's model, you can see that culture has a profound effect on each of us. As a culturally competent manager, you will recognize that culture determines why your employees

- prefer authoritarian or democratic leadership
- need more or less personal space and privacy
- perceive punctuality as important or not
- are future-oriented or look to the past
- are factual or intuitive in decision making
- value individual achievement or loyalty to the group
- focus on the words or on everything except the words

When observing employee conflicts, other managers may not notice that the underlying issue could be cultural. They might think, "What's wrong with you? You shouldn't be so upset." But if you are a culturally competent manager you will recognize that cultural background strongly influences the way employees respond to any situation. Once you understand how pervasive a person's culture is and how different it may be from yours, you will appreciate the complexity of good management in our highly competitive global marketplace. Effective managers see and accept things as others see and accept them.

Cultural differences can affect work relationships in domestic as well as multinational corporations. Subcultures in the United States, often labeled by geographic region, may affect workers' behavior, communication style, and values just as much as national cultures do. Understanding your workforce includes recognizing and respecting the cultural roots of their attributes, whether international or domestic, and trying to adapt to their culturally-based values and behaviors. As a culturally competent manager, you will take better advantage of this type of diversity and see it as an asset to be valued, not a liability to be discouraged.

Barriers to Cultural Competence

The biggest roadblock to cultural competence is our own cultural values. From an early age, we are taught that our way of doing things is the right way, and everyone who is different is wrong. This bias against difference is natural and normal, not pathological, and mostly subconscious. But every day our biases determine what we see and how we judge those around us. We have biases about almost every dimension of human identity.

> Bias is a normal psychological reaction to difference.

We are attracted to and tend to like people who are similar to us, not different from us. The perceived similarities may or may not be real. When people think they're similar, they expect to have positive future interactions. Therefore, the discovery of similarities and differences is crucial in developing relationships. Here's how it works:

Think about a time you had to interview a job candidate. When the candidate walked in and greeted you, you immediately noticed their gender, race, dress, appearance, speech patterns, handshake, and even body size. And you immediately formed judgments based on those outward factors. If you perceived those factors to be similar to yours, you probably formed a positive impression of the candidate. If you perceived those factors to be different from yours, you probably formed a negative impression. As the interview went along and you gained more information about their background, experiences, and skills, you probably paid the most attention to the information that confirmed your first impressions and disregarded the information that conflicted with your first impressions. That normal mental process can lead to bias and discrimination. It can also lead to costly hiring mistakes.

Overcoming the Barriers

How can you avoid scenarios like the one above? Howard Ross, the founder of Cook Ross, an international diversity consulting company and author of *Everyday Bias* and *Reinventing Diversity*, suggests four strategies for developing cultural competence:

1 *Recognize and accept that you have biases.* Bias is a normal psychological phenomenon. Rather than feel guilty about your biases, take responsibility for them. Once you accept them, you can begin to limit their impact.
2 *Practice "constructive uncertainty."* Slow down decision making, especially when it affects other people.
3 *Try to interact regularly with and learn about people you feel biased against.* Exposing yourself to positive role models will reduce the risk of discrimination.
4 *Look at how you make decisions.* Consider the impact of environmental factors, time of day, and your physical and emotional state in order to identify barriers to perception.[xvi]

Strategies for developing cultural competence:

1 Recognize and accept that you have biases
2 Practice constructive uncertainty
3 Learn about people that you feel biased against
4 Look at how you make decisions

Let's apply Ross's four strategies to the job interview scenario described earlier. If your first impression of the candidate is negative because you perceived their outward characteristics (age, appearance, race, gender, voice, handshake) to be different from yours, what should you do? The first step is to recognize your bias and the possibility of premature judgment. Next, deliberately decide that you won't jump to conclusions. Ask questions and listen closely to the responses. Try to penetrate well below the surface so you can exchange information more accurately. Bring in another interviewer whose opinions you respect and then compare impressions afterward.

It's true that similarities make it easier to build relationships at work. It's also true that most work groups develop their own subculture over time; members adapt their values, behaviors, attitudes, and even appearance so they fit into the workgroup and gain a sense of belonging. However, different traits and outlooks will give your team balance, opportunities for growth, and possibilities for learning new ways of thinking. Becoming aware of your mental processes will help you to become culturally competent so you can make better decisions, whether it's about hiring or anything else. You will read more about these processes in Chapter 4.

A Case Study of Corporate Cultural Competence

After examining the roots of cultural differences and what's involved in becoming culturally competent, let's look more closely at how a very high-profile corporation responds to its multicultural environments.

Honda Motor Company is one of the most successful multinational companies in the world, employing 140,000 people globally. Astonishingly, Honda has been profitable every year since its inception in 1949. The Honda business model, known as lean manufacturing, is built on Eastern principles that emphasize

- simplicity over complexity
- minimalism over waste
- a flat organization over a complex hierarchy
- perpetual change

Staying true to this cultural framework is the secret to the company's excellent performance. Just how does Honda do it? Jeffrey Rothfeder spent five years researching the company and describes in his book, *Driving Honda*, how the organization's processes align with their bedrock principles. Take one of these principles, for example – "respect individualism." Given the Japanese culture's emphasis on teamwork, this principle is surprising. Most companies encourage workers to team up toward a common goal. But Honda views collaboration from the vantage point of the individual, not the team. Honda sees the individual's capabilities, decision-making, knowledge, and creativity as the source of the group's performance. In short, Honda practices cultural competence.

This quote from the founder, Soichiro Honda, captures the profound respect for individualism:

> "In the ocean you see a bunch of fish and they're going every which way. And something happens, a stimulus happens where one lines up, then another, and another, until they all line up and they go together in

the same direction, perfectly. Later, they separate again to find their own way and nourishment. That's also how successful teams and businesses work."[xvii]

This emphasis on individualism and creativity translates into physical aspects of the workplace. Honda factories are flat environments. The offices are open bullpens with desks; there are no private dining rooms -just a cafeteria, and no reserved parking spaces. Employees have no job descriptions. The result, according to Rothfeder, is enthusiastic, efficient, productive workplaces with high morale and frequent communication.

The Honda case demonstrates that maintaining a consistent corporate culture and being sensitive to the cultural environment are fundamental aspects of business success.

Culture and Communication Style

At this point you may be thinking, "All this sounds true enough; it goes along with what I've seen in my own career. But the concept of cultural competence is pretty abstract. My job description doesn't cover establishing and maintaining the organization's culture. What are some concrete actions I can take when communicating that will enhance my cultural competence and help the company to succeed?"

The answer begins with recognizing that every day, when you interact with coworkers, team members, customers, suppliers, and other stakeholders, their culture acts as a lens through which your messages are filtered. Similarly, their messages to you are filtered through your own cultural lens. Becoming aware of unintended distortions of a message's meanings is the first step toward cultural competency.

> Cultural competence is reflected in communication style.

Next, you can become conscious of specific ways that culture influences communication behaviors, including these:

- Whether messages are given directly or indirectly
- The amount of personal information shared in conversations
- The amount of silence that is comfortable
- The voice volume and nonverbal expressiveness
- The amount of formality or informality in messages

- The use of eye contact when giving or receiving messages
- The amount of space between people or the use of touch when communicating

Naoki Kameda, a prominent Japanese business communication researcher, applied these concepts to a multi-cultural workplace interaction. It is a conversation between a Chinese police officer in Hong Kong and his English supervisor:

Chinese police officer: My mother is not well, sir.
English supervisor: So?
Chinese police officer: She has to go into hospital.
English supervisor: Well?
Chinese police officer: On Thursday, sir.

According to Kameda, the meaning of this exchange is clouded by cultural differences in communication style. The Chinese officer is hoping that his boss will realize what he wants and offer this before he has to ask for it. In British English, however, it is more typical to start with the request and then give reasons if required. So, the English version of this conversation would be something like this:

Chinese police officer: Could I take a day off, please?
English supervisor: Why?
Chinese police officer: My mother is not well and must go to the hospital.[xviii]

Typical British English speech patterns are similar to US English patterns in their degree of directness. When people from Asian cultures are more indirect, Westerners may view them as being evasive. A Westerner lacking cultural competence might impatiently prod the speaker to "get to the point." On the other hand, a culturally competent Westerner would understand that the Asian roundabout pattern is used to avoid the risk of hurt feelings and is therefore often a more relationship-sensitive communication style.

Kameda concluded that the indirect communication style represents important values, based on the "3Hs":

- Humanity – warm consideration for others
- Harmony – efforts not to hurt the feelings of others
- Humility – modesty[xix]

By comparison, a direct style seems pretty self-centered, doesn't it?

Culturally Competent Communication and Empathy

It's easier to communicate with others when you understand and agree with the cultural values behind their communication style preferences. Furthermore, if you can empathize with the other person, share their feelings, and relate to their intentions, then you might even adopt their communication style during the interaction. All you have to do is ask yourself, "If I were on the receiving end, how would I react to this message?" Then adjust your communication style so the receiver's understanding is closer to what you intended. As you will read in Chapter 5, effective business communication leads to stronger relationships and feelings of empathy and trust. These emotional conditions, in turn, lead to improved performance, productivity, and organizational success.

> "Successful business communication is about 10% business and 90% human relations."
>
> A. Wilson, 1975

How to Improve Your Intercultural Communication

Here are some strategies that you can use when communicating with your multi-cultural work group:

- Ask each person about how they interpreted a specific message.
- Identify the cultural influences on each person and brainstorm ways that people can accommodate one another.
- Plan communication with the work group's cultures in mind so that everyone can understand.
- Encourage people to consider the impact of culture when interpreting messages, and to seek clarification rather than making assumptions.[xx]

How Your Employees Can Improve Their Intercultural Communication

Here are some strategies that you can encourage your multi-cultural work group to use when communicating with each other:

- Remember that everyone has a culture that affects how they interact with others. Be aware of your own beliefs, implicit biases, and assumptions. Think about how they might influence the way you interact with others.

- Avoid assumptions. Acknowledge differences, but don't make assumptions about people based on those differences. Stereotypes can lead to misunderstandings.
- Be open to new ways of doing things and listen to others' perspectives. Diverse viewpoints can help you understand a problem in a new way or offer a unique solution to a problem.
- Use respectful communication practices when sharing feedback.
- Be careful with humor. People from different cultural backgrounds have different views on what is funny or acceptable.

Summary

Along with appreciation for DEIA principles, cultural competence is a cornerstone for getting along, getting it done, and getting ahead at work. Culturally competent managers understand that culture profoundly affects workplace behavior and attitudes, and they know how to navigate relevant cultural differences in order to maximize workers' loyalty, satisfaction, productivity, and the bottom line.

While bias against difference is natural and normal, it can restrict thinking and prevent the development of workplace relationships, empathy, and trust. Culturally competent managers recognize that culture is a lens that filters messages. They develop flexible communication styles to overcome barriers and increase shared meaning.

Notes

i   Hart Research Associates (2013). *It Takes More than a Major: Employer Priorities for College Learning and Student Success* (Washington, DC: Association of American Colleges and Universities).

ii Mark Murphy (2021). "Why New Hires Fail." *Leadership IQ* Blog. Retrieved from https://www.leadershipiq.com/blogs/leadershipiq/35354241-why-new-hires-fail-emotional-intelligence-vs-skills

iii David Bolchover (2012). "Competing Across Borders: How Cultural and Communication Barriers Affect Business." *The Economist Intelligence Unit Ltd.* Report, p. 11.

iv Norm Sigband and Arthur Bell (1986). *Communicating for Management and Business*, 4th ed. (Glenview, IL: Scott Foresman), pp. 69–70.

v   Nairan Ramirez-Esparza, Samuel D. Gosling, Veronica Benet-Martinez, Jeffrey P. Potter, and James W. Pennebaker (2006). "Do Bilinguals have Two Personalities? A Special Case of Cultural Frame Switching." *Journal of Research in Personality*, Vol. 40, pp. 99–120.

vi Richard Nisbett (2004). *The Geography of Thought: How Asians and Westerners Think Differently … and Why.* (Free Press).

vii Malcolm Gladwell (2008). *Outliers: The Story of Success* (New York: Little, Brown and Company), p. 175.

viii Geert Hofstede (1980, Summer). "Motivation, Leadership and Organization: Do American Theories Apply Abroad?" *Organizational Dynamics,* pp. 42–63.

ix Hofstede, "Motivation, Leadership and Organization," p. 51.

x Hofstede, "Motivation, Leadership and Organization," p. 51.

xi Hofstede, "Motivation, Leadership and Organization," p. 51.

xii Geert Hofstede and Associates (1998). *Masculinity and Femininity: The Taboo Dimension of National Cultures* (Thousand Oaks, CA: SAGE), p. 37.

xiii Hofstede, "Motivation, Leadership and Organization", p. 52.

xiv Erin Meyer (2015). *The Culture Map: Breaking Through the Invisible Boundaries of Global Business* (New York: Public Affairs), pp. 219–242.

xv Richard Conrad (2019). *Culture Hacks: Deciphering Differences in American, Chinese, and Japanese Thinking* (Lioncrest Publishing), pp. 14.

xvi Howard J. Ross (2014, August 3). "An Appeal to Our Inner Judge." *The New York Times,* p. D3.

xvii Jeffrey Rothfelder (2014). *Driving Honda: Inside the World's Most Innovative Car Company* (New York: Portfolio/Penguin), p. 134.

xviii This example is from A. Kirkpatrick (2009). *World Englishes: Implications for International Communication and English Language Teaching.* (Cambridge, England: Cambridge University Press) as reported in Naoki Kameda (2014). "Japanese Business Discourse of Oneness: A Personal Perspective." *International Journal of Business Communication,* Vol. 51, no. 1, pp. 93–113.

xix Naoki Kameda (2014). "Japanese Business Discourse of Oneness: A Personal Perspective." *International Journal of Business Communication,* Vol. 51, no. 1, p. 102.

xx Patient Centered Outcomes Research Institute (2020). "Building Effective Multi-Stakeholder Research Teams." Retrieved April 17, 2022, from https://research-teams.pcori.org/stakeholders#Practicing%20Effective%20Team%20Communication

Chapter 3

The Sequence for Success Model

Chapter 1 introduced the first cornerstone or basic concept of this book: *diversity appreciation*. Chapter 1 documented the increasing diversity of the workforce and explained why diversity is a competitive advantage for organizations. Chapter 2 introduced the second cornerstone: *cultural competence*. Chapter 2 showed how profound differences in employees' cultural values, customs, and communication patterns require managers to be skillful in navigating these differences. Culturally competent managers know how to develop positive relationships with diverse employees that will positively affect workers' loyalty, satisfaction, and productivity.

In this chapter we build on these two cornerstones (Figure 3.1) to create a framework for the rest of the book. This chapter, which completes Part I, suggests that managers who value diversity, equity, inclusion, and accessibility and who are culturally competent will get along (Part II), get it done (Part III), and get ahead (Part IV).

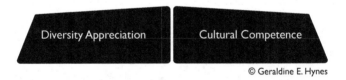

© Geraldine E. Hynes

Figure 3.1 Cornerstones of the Sequence for Success.

Interpersonal Communication and Interpersonal Relationships

Getting along with peers, direct reports, bosses, customers, suppliers, and shareholders is mostly a matter of communication. To build strong relationships with all these constituencies you must interact with them regularly. As you will read in Chapter 4, there can be no relationship if there is

DOI: 10.4324/9781003335177-4

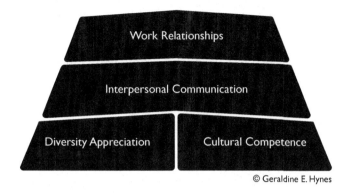

© Geraldine E. Hynes

Figure 3.2 Building Blocks of the Sequence for Success.

no communication. Therefore, communication and work relationships are the first two building blocks for organizational success. We will set these building blocks on top of the two cornerstones already in place (Figure 3.2).

Let's think a little more about the impact of your interpersonal communication. If you're a manager, your daily interactions with your direct reports typically center on these ten topics, right?

1 Procedures
2 Guidance
3 Policies
4 Work conditions
5 Work problems
6 Solutions to work problems
7 Deadlines, goals
8 Corrective feedback
9 Positive feedback
10 Raises, promotions, advancement

You might want to add to this list of topics, depending on your unique situation at work, but these are the top ten things that managers and their staff talk about on the job. You already know that your communication style when interacting with your staff about these topics will significantly determine how well they do their job. Their performance depends on the clarity, accuracy, and timeliness of your instructions, information, and feedback.

But did you know that your communication style will also determine what they think about you as a boss? An interesting study of 363 adults with an average of eight years of work experience focused on what they considered to be a "good boss." Contrary to what you might predict, the researchers found no evidence that the workers evaluated their bosses according to how the bosses used their authority, control, or power. Instead, the most important factor for judging their bosses to be good or bad was the extent to which the bosses showed appreciation, respect, or high regard for the workers. This factor is called "affiliation." By the way, gender did not seem to influence the workers' ratings of the quality of their managers. Both male and female workers rated both male and female managers as "good" bosses if their communication was high on affiliation.[i]

> Good bosses are affiliative.

Making an effort to develop relationships with your employees will make your job easier. Ever wonder why they don't comply with your demands/ requests? After all, you are the boss. Here's why: your job title may give you authority, also known as position power, but if you want to influence your direct reports, you also need personal power. Personal power derives from your credibility. The elements of managerial credibility are:

- Rank – position in the hierarchy
- Expertise – skill or knowledge
- Image – personal attractiveness
- Common ground – shared value
- Goodwill – personal relationships

It's that last item on the bulleted list that we're talking about here. Goodwill is how you get your staff to put up with poor working conditions, long hours, stressful deadlines, and nasty customers. Goodwill is a product of personal relationships.

> Position power = authority
> Personal power = credibility

Relationships and Emotional Conditions

Let's add a third building block to our Sequence for Success model, one that captures key emotional conditions caused by strong relationships. "Wait. Why should I worry about emotions and relationships with my employees?" you might ask. "I have to work with these people, but I don't have to like them." True. In fact, if you ever find coworkers that you like well enough to become friends outside of work, that's a bonus. More often, however, the coworkers we consider to be our friends will disappear from our lives when they (or we) leave the organization.

On the other hand, a strong case can be made for trying to develop positive relationships with your team and your direct reports, so that certain emotional conditions occur. Among these key emotions are loyalty, satisfaction, commitment, and trust. They are represented by the new building block in Figure 3.3. Notice that "liking" is not on this list of emotions. You can trust people without liking them. You can also feel loyal, satisfied, and committed to a job without liking the actual work.

Organizational commitment means that your employees will:

- Identify with the organization's goals and values
- Want to belong to the organization
- Be willing to display effort on behalf of the organization[ii]

Research consistently shows that low organizational commitment leads to absenteeism, turnover, and unrest. On the other hand, high organizational commitment leads to trust, quality, and quantity of communication, involvement, and productivity.[iii] Therefore, if you treat your employees well, they will work harder for you.

© Geraldine E. Hynes

Figure 3.3 More Building Blocks of the Sequence for Success.

Emotional Conditions and Performance

Let's finish building the Sequence for Success model by adding a final building block that represents productivity and success, your organization's ultimate goals. The connection between job performance and key emotional conditions is well established. Figure 3.4 illustrates that when employees feel a sense of loyalty, commitment, job satisfaction, and trust, their productivity improves, and, ultimately, the organization succeeds.

Want more evidence for the truth of this Success model – that communication and commitment directly lead to organizational success? In 2013, the Project Management Institute published the results of their survey of 1,093 project managers, executives, and business owners who were involved in large capital projects worldwide. The business leaders agreed that *the most crucial success factor in project management is effective communication* to all

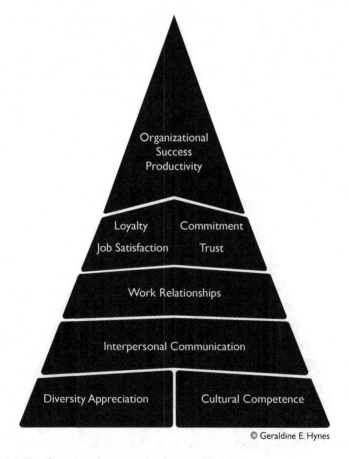

© Geraldine E. Hynes

Figure 3.4 The Complete Sequence for Success Model.

stakeholders. Further, the study showed that highly effective communicators are *five times* more likely to be high performers than poor communicators, as measured by whether they finished the project on time, within budget, and according to the original goals.[iv]

If you're still not convinced that managerial communication leads to organizational success, here's even more evidence. In a 2012 review of 263 research studies across 192 companies, Gallup found that companies in the top quartile for "engaged" employees, compared with the bottom quartile, had 22 percent higher profitability, 10 percent higher customer ratings, 28 percent less theft, and 48 percent fewer safety incidents.[v]

Employee Engagement

Employee engagement is a hot topic. Engaged workers are committed, involved, enthusiastic, and energized. Engaged workers typically are also high performers, according to a survey conducted by HR.com. Over 90 percent of the survey respondents believed that there is solid evidence linking engagement to performance, and that engagement is the factor that has the strongest impact on customer service and productivity.[vi]

> Engaged workers are committed, involved, enthusiastic, energized, and productive.

To employees, engagement means having a sense of purpose in their work. They want social and interpersonal connections with their colleagues and managers. They want to feel valued by their organizations and managers. They want meaningful – though not necessarily in-person – interactions, not just transactions.[vii] Today's managers acknowledge that the way people feel at work profoundly influences how they perform. If you think that pay is the primary influence on performance, you haven't been paying attention. Although financial rewards are relevant – who among us would work for free? – the psychological and emotional rewards are what keep us on the job.

Well, then, what drives engagement? In a word, communication. The Great Place To Work Institute found that employees enjoy working in an environment where they "trust the people they work for, have pride in what they do and enjoy the people they work with."[viii] Such positive work environments are typically characterized by open communication. While larger companies may expect their Communication Department to be responsible for broadcasting information internally and externally, most employees consider their managers to be the most important source of transparency. Managers are expected to share relevant information with direct reports; managers are responsible for promoting a sense of belonging and commitment, and helping their employees to understand the company's mission. These behaviors develop trust, which leads to employee engagement.[ix]

And yet, in the HR.com survey of, only 40 percent of respondents said their managers prioritize employee engagement, and just 28 percent said their managers are highly skilled at fostering engaged individuals and teams.[x] Clearly, most employers still face major employee engagement challenges.

Facilitating Engagement through Communication

Step back for a minute so you can get the big picture and see where you are now. We started by acknowledging that today's workforce is incredibly diverse and that managers must be sensitive to the cultural differences that people bring to the workplace. Upon those two cornerstones we built a model for success. The model illustrates that daily interpersonal communication leads to stronger relationships. Those relationships cause certain emotional conditions – trust, loyalty, commitment, and job satisfaction. These important emotions motivate people to work harder and be more productive, which ultimately leads to the organization's success.

The most important implication of our Sequence for Success model is that managers must facilitate open, honest, and frequent communication. "Wait a minute," you might object. "If people are spending all their time talking, when are they going to get the job done?" While you may be tempted to tell workers to quiet down and get to work, discouraging employees from interacting with you or each other will backfire. Employees need to feel safe to speak up, ask questions, challenge ideas, own their mistakes, and try out new ideas. Only then will you have an environment of highly engaged employees where issues can be freely discussed and innovation can flourish.[xi]

Companies that realize their workers are more productive if they have more social interaction are taking some simple steps to foster internal communication. Here are some examples. Bank of America observed that employees working in their call centers who had formed tight-knit communications groups were more productive and less likely to quit. To increase social communication, the bank introduced a shared 15-minute coffee break each day. Afterward, call-handling productivity increased by more than 10 percent, and turnover declined by nearly 70 percent.

In a second case, a pharmaceutical company replaced coffee makers used by a few marketing workers with a larger cafe area. The result? Increased sales and less turnover. A third example is from a tech company. The workers who sat at larger tables in the cafeteria, thus communicating more, were found to be more productive than workers who sat at smaller tables.[xii]

Adam Grant, an organizational psychologist, presents a fourth example of a company that facilitates communication. In his book, *Give and Take: A Revolutionary Approach to Success*, Grant describes a large telecommunications firm in San Francisco. The professional engineers who worked at the firm were asked to rate themselves and each other on how much time they spent giving and receiving information from one another. The results reinforce the connection between communication and productivity. The engineers who gave the most help were the most productive and were held in the highest respect by their peers. By giving often, engineers built up more trust and attracted more cooperation from across their work groups, not just from the people they helped.[xiii]

In his book, Grant also tells how a former CEO at Deloitte improved his communication style. The executive, Jim Quigley, set a goal in meetings to talk no more than 20 percent of the time. "One of my objectives is listening. Many times you can have a bigger impact if you know what to ask rather than knowing what to say," Quigley explained. As he increased his questions, Quigley found himself gaining a deeper understanding of other people's needs.[xiv]

As you can see from these examples, simple steps such as arranging the work environment to facilitate communication and encouraging people to interact informally will pay big dividends. Talking, listening, and asking questions are learning experiences. Enjoyable learning experiences. The more you learn about your employees and the more they learn about each other, the easier it is for everyone to work together toward a common goal. That's the key to managerial success.

Talking, listening, and asking questions are learning experiences.

Summary

This chapter presents a model that is the framework for the book's premise. Beginning with the two cornerstones of diversity appreciation and cultural competence that are described in Chapters 1 and 2, this chapter shows that managerial communication should be frequent, open, and honest. Frequent, respectful interactions with peers, bosses, direct reports, and other stakeholders will result in stronger work relationships. These relationships, in turn, will foster the key emotional conditions of trust, loyalty, commitment, and job satisfaction. People feeling these emotions will be engaged in their work. They will be motivated to work cooperatively, which leads to productivity and organizational success. Managers who understand this sequence will be able to get along, get it done, and get ahead.

Notes

i L. McWorthy, and D.D. Henningsen (2014). "Looking at Favorable and Unfavorable Superior-Subordinate Relationships through Dominance and Affiliation Lenses," *International Journal of Business Communication* Vol. 51, no. 2, pp. 123–37.

ii M. Shafiq, M. Zia-ur-Rehman, and M. Rashid (2013). "Impact of Compensation, Training and Development and Supervisory Support on Organizational Commitment," *Compensation and Benefits Review,* Vol. 45, no. 5, pp. 278–85.

iii O. Hargie, D. Tourish, and N. Wilson (2001). "Communication Audits and the Effects of Increased Information: A Follow-Up Study," *Journal of Business Communication* 39, no. 4, pp. 414–36. See also G.F. T. R. Zolin, and J.L. Hartman (2009). "The Central Role of Communication in Developing Trust and Its Effect on Employee Involvement," *Journal of Business Communication,* Vol. 46, no. 3, pp. 287–310.

iv Project Management Institute, Inc. (2013). "The High Cost of Low Performance: The Essential Role of Communications" (Pulse of the Profession In-depth Report), Retrieved from www.pmi.org

v T. Schwartz, and C. Porath (2014, June 1). "Why You Hate Work," *New York Times*, p. 1SR.

vi HR Research Institute (2018). "The State of Employee Engagement in 2018: Leverage leadership and culture to maximize engagement." Retrieved from https://www.hr.com/en/resources/free_research_white_papers/the-state-of-employee-engagement-in-2018-mar2018_jeqfvgoq.html

vii A. DeSmet, B. Dowling, M. Mugayar-Baldocchi, and B. Schanninger (2021). "'Great Attrition' or 'Great Attraction'? The Choice is Yours." *McKinsey Quarterly.* Retrieved from https://www.mckinsey.com/business-functions/people-and-organizational-performance/our-insights/great-attrition-or-great-attraction-the-choice-is-yours

viii A.B. Carroll (2006, July 29). "Trust is the Key When Rating Great Workplaces," Retrieved from http://onlineathens.com/stories/073006/business_20060730047.shtml, p. 1.

ix K. Mishra, L. Boynton, and A. Mishra (2014). "Driving Employee Engagement: The Expanded Role of Internal Communications," *International Journal of Business Communication,* Vol. 51, no. 2, pp. 183–202.

x HR Research Institute, 2018.

xi J. Peters (2019). *Employee Engagement: Creating High Positive Energy at Work* (Randburg, South Africa: KR Publishing), p. 57.

xii S. Lohr (2014, June 21). "Unblinking Eyes Track Employees: Workplace Surveillance Sees Good and Bad," *New York Times,* Retrieved from http://www.nytimes.com/2014/06/22/technology/workplace-surveillance-sees-good-and-bad.html?_r=0

xiii A. Grant (2013). *Give and Take: A Revolutionary Approach to Success* (New York, NY: Viking Press), pp. 58–9.

xiv Grant, p. 265.

Part II

Get Along

Chapter 4

Strategies for Finding Out What's Going On

As discussed in Part I of this book, the daily interactions that you engage in upward, downward, laterally, and diagonally along the organizational hierarchy will determine your success. The Sequence for Success model (Figure 4.1) shows that interpersonal communication is the first step in the sequence that culminates in organizational success. That's because communication leads to relationships; relationships foster important emotional conditions such as loyalty, job satisfaction, and commitment; and in turn, these emotional conditions trigger effective work performance. The more people engage in an organization's life, the more connected they become and the more effective the organization becomes. The communication strategies for "getting along" will enable you to "get it done" and ultimately to "get ahead."

Part II focuses on the daily conversational behaviors that will help you "get along" with coworkers, employees, and bosses. This chapter describes a range of communication strategies that will keep you informed about the people and events in your work environment. Chapter 5 describes communication strategies that will build stronger work relationships. The relationship level is where most of the work gets done. It's also where you experience most of the difficulties.

A key concept in the relationship process is the notion of emotional intelligence (EI). The next section explains this concept and its relevance.

Emotional Intelligence

How good are you at staying calm under pressure at work? When others complain to you, do you show empathy even though deep down you may feel that they are just whining? Do your coworkers think you are easy to get along with? Is it easy to socialize with your team?

Such behaviors reflect social and emotional competence. Popularly known as EI, social and emotional competence has been shown to be a better predictor of professional success than cognitive intelligence or specialized knowledge.[1] In fact, research shows that EI accounts for an amazing

DOI: 10.4324/9781003335177-6

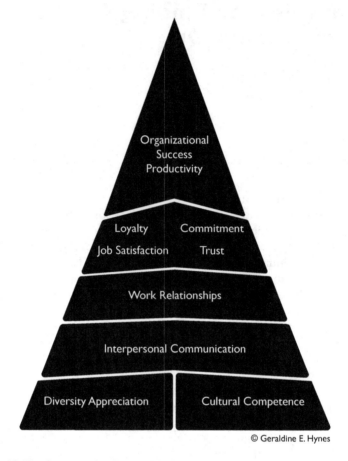

© Geraldine E. Hynes

Figure 4.1 The Sequence for Success Model.

58 percent of performance in all job types. Furthermore, 90 percent of high job performers are also high in EI, yet only 20 percent of low job performers are high in EI.[ii]

> Emotional intelligence is the ability to recognize, understand, and respond to emotions in ourselves and others.

Research focusing on business leaders shows that EI scores are the highest for middle managers but lowest for executives. In trying to explain that difference, the researchers observed that executives are more likely to be promoted because of what they know or how long they have worked, rather than for their management skills or social awareness. However, high EI executives are the best performers.[iii]

Briefly, EI is defined as the ability to recognize, understand, and respond to emotions in ourselves and others. Unlike personality, which remains stable throughout most of our lives, EI can be improved with training. By improving our ability to recognize and understand emotions, we can do a much better job of managing our behavior and our social interactions.[iv] Daniel Goleman's landmark book about EI lists six ways people can cope with workplace pressures and the resulting stress on relationships. These competencies are generally accepted as the starting point for emotion management. They include the ability to:

1   Become self-aware in managing emotions and controlling impulses
2   Set goals and perform well
3   Be motivated and creative
4   Empathize with others
5   Handle relationships effectively
6   Develop appropriate social skills[v]

Mastering these competencies will greatly affect the way you interact with everyone in the workplace.

In their book, *Emotional Intelligence 2.0*, Bradberry and Greaves offer many practical suggestions for improving your self-awareness, managing yourself, becoming more socially aware, and managing relationships in all aspects of life. Here are some highlights that apply to workplace relationships:

1   During meetings, use people's names. Recognizing someone by name acknowledges them as individuals and opens a channel for communication. It serves to both affirm and identify the nature of the relationship.
2   Don't take too many notes, but use nonverbal behaviors (looking, nodding) to indicate that you are paying attention as you listen.
3   When interacting with culturally diverse people, be open, respectful, sincere, and curious.
4   During disagreements, acknowledge the other person's point or feelings before stating your own opinion. Be willing to offer a "fix it" statement no matter who is right.
5   When interacting with lower-status employees, use compliments liberally, and always be pleasant and courteous.
6   Have tough conversations instead of letting problems fester.
7   When things explode, under-react until you have learned more.
8   Get real value out of every social interaction, even with people you don't like.

In short, some degree of self-awareness and emotional intelligence contributes positively to your success in collaborative work groups. You need to be aware of your impact on others as well as your own areas of sensitivity and vulnerability.[vi] Social and emotional competence will smooth your everyday interactions on the job. That's how you'll be able to stay in the loop.

Next, we take a closer look at vertical interactions – those between you and your direct reports. "That seems easy enough," you may be thinking. "I tell them what they need to know, and they tell me what I need to know." Well, maybe it is easy to share information when it's neutral or positive. But conversations are tougher between you and your employees when expressing differences and when bad news is involved. Are your conversations about negative topics a matter of, "I tell them what they need to know, and they tell me what they think I want to hear"? If so, read on.

Communicating Bad News

A typical tough conversation is the one in which you must give your workgroup information they don't want to hear. Any change in policy or procedure is generally unwelcome simply because it is a change. Employees are comfortable with the status quo, despite a tendency to complain about the way things are. When a crisis triggers a change in policy or procedure, the result is often negative – layoffs, reductions in compensation, relocations, increases in workload, elimination of breaks or downtime. It's important for companies to announce bad news without damaging the work culture. The worst that can happen at this point is that the communication channel in your functional area closes up.

The COVID-19 pandemic that began in 2020 reshaped almost every organization, triggering many examples of bad news messages that risked damaging the work culture. A major challenge for most companies was to communicate the rapidly evolving transformations while maintaining morale, trust, and productivity. These efforts were especially problematic as workers became isolated at home, reducing interaction among colleagues and placing camaraderie and peer support at risk.

A model case study of an organization that responded successfully to COVID-19 challenges is the Department of Psychiatry at Brigham and Women's Hospital, Boston, Massachusetts. Innovative processes were quickly implemented for communicating with frontline clinical teams (physicians, nurses, medical assistants, and social workers) to prevent burnout during the pandemic. The interventions maintained trust, achieved values alignment, and strengthened the workplace culture.

Let's take a closer look at some of those communication strategies. First, a daily COVID-19 emergency planning update was emailed to all members of the department. This change significantly consolidated the number of emails employees received on a daily basis. Second, the chair of the department also emailed all members of the department on a weekly basis. These messages provided realistic yet uplifting assessments, adopted a conversational tone, and minimized organizational distance. Third, team leaders continued all regular administrative meetings via Zoom videoconferencing. Fourth, virtual huddles enabled leaders to provide frequent updates, announce upcoming changes, and optimize collaboration, preventing the formation of silos. Fifth, virtual town hall events organized by division chiefs and attended by the chair provided support for members of the department to discuss concerns and questions. The chat function of Microsoft Teams for these events ensured two-way communication.

Perhaps the hospital's most innovative communication strategy was the establishment of virtual peer support groups, which created niche forums for employees to articulate their needs and connect with one another. An example of such a peer support group is a mothers' group. The group meets weekly to discuss topics including the highs and lows of parenting in the age of COVID-19. Participants also collaborate on ways to promote professional equity for women.

The Brigham and Women's Hospital case exemplifies how organizations can survive crises by establishing formal and informal communication channels that assure transparency, a key for reducing burnout. Clear, consistent, and sincere strategies facilitate a two-way flow of information and decision making, while mirroring value for the team.[vii]

Moving from the organizational level to the individual level, let's explore a strategy that you as a manager can easily adopt when communicating negative messages. The underlying principle of this strategy is that the message's organization will impact the receivers' reaction as much as the message's content will. Although some situations call for a direct structure, tactfully written bad news messages generally should follow this indirect organizational pattern:

Format for a bad news message:

- Buffer
- Reasons
- Bad news
- Goodwill

1   Begin with a buffer. Typical buffers are a compliment ("Good job defusing that angry client yesterday, Ben"), statement of appreciation ("Thanks for taking my call"), agreement on a principle ("Safety is our

top priority"), or a shared goal ("We're out to bury Eldridge"). This opening establishes a positive, or at least neutral, connection.

2   Give reasons for the upcoming change. Presenting background information, facts, and incidents will help your receivers to understand what's behind the decision.

3   Deliver the bad news. By now the employees are prepared. They won't like what they hear, but they'll know why they are hearing it. Stick to the facts as you know them. Avoid sharing your doubts and other negative emotions, because feelings are contagious and they'll take their cue from you.

4   End with goodwill. Express confidence in their ability to weather the change and reassure them that you'll remain at their side, supporting and keeping them informed throughout the transition.

Receiving Bad News

If you're like most bosses, you're probably insulated from the truth. When you ask your people how they are, they say "Fine" and "Things are going great." So how do you find out what's really going on and what you need to fix?

One communication strategy to encourage candid information is the "Triple Two." Ask what two things you should stop doing, two things you should start doing, and two things you need to keep doing. That gives your people permission to speak freely. Asking for honest feedback makes it easier for your direct reports to go beyond what they think you want to hear.[viii] The Triple Two also works when you want to repair strained relationships with colleagues and coworkers who you think might be withholding important information.

Of course, it's important that you be authentic about asking employees to give you the straight talk. If you punish them for telling you something you don't want to hear or fail to act on any of their input, they will stop telling you anything. And that's a recipe for failure. The next paragraphs offer suggestions for ways to respond to negative feedback. We begin with saying you're sorry.

Apologizing

When you have messed up and your team wants you to make amends, there's a right way and a wrong way to apologize. The wrong way is to use the word, "but." "I'm sorry I hurt your feelings, but ... " denies wrong-doing. It also indicates that you aren't really apologizing. Instead, to diffuse anger and resentment, try the "MIDAS" strategy:

M = admit you made a **M**istake
I = admit you caused **I**njury
D = explain what you'll **D**o differently
A = say how you'll make **A**mends
S = **S**top talking[ix]

Research shows that in many situations, the "M" and the "I" count more than the "D" with the people you offended. That is, they might not expect you – or even want you to – do anything differently. They simply want you to admit wrongdoing. Much of the research on the effects of apologies has focused on the health care profession. In the past, medical professionals were reluctant to apologize to patients for fear that it would be interpreted as admitting fault, which would open them up to malpractice suits. Similarly, in business settings, corporate legal counsel has often urged against apologies because of the link to liability and the threat of lawsuits. Surprisingly, however, medical professionals who apologized have actually seen lower rates of malpractice claims.

Nonverbally, when apologizing, be sure to use the gestures, posture, and eye contact that you would like the offended person to use. If you behave positively and calmly, you will influence the other person's reaction.

Cultural Differences in Responding to Bad News

Not everything your employees tell you requires an apology. But they do expect some sort of response. As discussed in Part I of this book, trusting relationships are built on continuous communication, on two-way interactions. Therefore, when you ask what's going on and they tell you, you are usually expected to respond.

Your first response to bad news may be denial or defense. It's natural to react negatively to negative information, especially when you feel threatened. But as a manager, showing empathy in bad news situations will go far to create and maintain open channels. Once empathy is established, you can move on to an exploration of solutions. Sometimes they don't have solutions, but in a surprising number of situations, they do, and it's wise to listen to them.

Culture can affect the exchange of feelings and ideas, problems, and solutions. Various cultures view feedback differently. For example, as discussed in Chapter 2, workers in Western cultures prefer direct communication and expect honest feedback. In Eastern cultures, on the other hand, workers prefer a more indirect communication style and feedback that is subtle rather than blunt. In Eastern cultures, silence is respected. Silence, rather than talk, communicates. As a result, when working with people from Asian cultures, managers can benefit from learning to use silence as a type of response.[x] Even if you "know for sure" what someone is going to say, be patient and let them complete their thoughts. Rather than assuming, an open attitude will help you see the other person's side of a situation and strengthen the working relationship.

Strategies for Checking Understanding

David Eagleman is a neuroscientist at Stanford University, host of Emmy-nominated PBS/BBC series "The Brain," and author of several books. In his 2015 TED Talk he explained that we take in external data through our senses (principally seeing and hearing), but our brains process the meanings of that data by comparing it to what we've previously experienced and stored away in our memories. When you are looking out at your office or coworkers, you are not seeing what you think you are. What you think is reality is a fabricated construction because your eyes can't deliver enough visual information for your brain to build a picture in your head. So, your brain blends prior memories stored in your visual cortex to supplement the live streaming information coming from your eyes. Eagleman estimates the ratio is 80 percent from your memory and 20 percent live from your eyes. This is especially true when you're looking at something new. And that's why the typical outcome of any communication is, to some real degree, miscommunication.[xi]

> The typical outcome of any communication is miscommunication.

An inappropriate reaction will shut the channel immediately when you're on the receiving end of a message. This section presents three strategies for keeping the channel open, so you can stay informed and bring your perceptions closer to reality. The strategies are listening, reading nonverbals, and asking questions. These three strategies are especially critical when the information coming your way is negative. Applying the strategies also will strengthen your rapport with the speaker.

Listening

As a business professional, you probably spend half to two-thirds of your time listening, yet 75–90 percent of what you hear is ignored, misunderstood, or forgotten.[xii] That's because listening takes hard work. It's not a passive experience. Your brain is not a sponge that absorbs whatever comes along. Listening is especially difficult when you're busy and distracted with work. Your brain can think at least four times faster than anyone can talk, so while you're waiting for someone to get to the point, you've mentally moved on.

But if you listen deeply you can transcend the differences that exist between you and others. If you are perceived as a good listener, you can positively impact your employees' job satisfaction and reduce turnover intentions. Deep listening requires openness and empathy.[xiii]

To create a healthy work atmosphere you have to keep the communication channel open. Begin by physically and psychologically preparing yourself to listen:

1   Pick the best place. While it is not always possible to change the place, don't overlook better facilities when available. Selecting the best place helps reduce internal and external noise.
2   Pick the best time. As with place, it is not always possible to change the time. However, because time influences the psychological barriers of motivation, emotion, and willingness, deciding when to meet may significantly alter the conversation's outcome.
3   Think about personal biases that may be present. If you are unaware of personal bias, you may become selective and hear only what you want to hear. Emotional words can also trigger listener bias. Such phrases as "typical humorless accountant," "we tried that before, and it didn't work," or "all engineers think alike" can lead to negative emotional responses. The danger in such phrases is that they cause a listener to pay attention only to certain parts of a message. Don't let bias distract you from understanding the message.

Interesting research shows that men and women have different listening styles. When women listen, they tend to focus on the relationship. When they process information, their goal is to zoom in on emotions and moods. In an effort to relay support, women are often willing to allow others to open up and reveal what they care about. By contrast, men tend to listen for facts and information and are often less comfortable handling emotional content. They tend to be more interested in power and control, and they listen for solutions more often than for empathy.[xiv]

In interactive listening situations, you are expected not only to receive but also to respond to what the other person has said. An easy-to-remember formula for an effective response is ACE – Affirm, Comment, Expand.

Respond with the ACE Formula:

1   Affirm
2   Comment
3   Expand

Begin your response by *affirming* what you have heard the other person say. You accomplish this with a paraphrase, which reflects their meaning as you understood it rather than their exact words. After proving that you got the message, you can *comment* on it by saying whether you agree or disagree. Next you *expand* by explaining why you agree or disagree, adding your own two cents to the discussion. Following the ACE formula will lower any barriers and encourage the other person to be receptive and open to your opinions and ideas.

Reading Nonverbals

The old saying that a picture speaks a thousand words is still true. How you look and how you sound contribute more to the impression you create than what you say. Therefore, when your coworkers, bosses, and direct reports are sending messages, it's important to show attention with your whole body, not just your words.

Similarly, whenever you send messages to others at work, the receivers will be reading your nonverbals. They will judge you on two dimensions: *competence* and *warmth*. Competence gets to how smart, able, and skilled your receivers think you are. Warmth is about how nice, engaging, and friendly they think you are. Obviously, for maximum success in communication, the goal is to demonstrate both competence and warmth through your nonverbal behavior. The problem is that, typically, as confidence goes up, warmth goes down.

Here are some easy-to-adopt nonverbal behaviors that will help you project both competence and warmth nonverbally, whether you are speaking or listening. First, practice eye contact with everyone in the room. Avoid sweeping back and forth with your eyes like a windshield wiper, but instead hold eye contact with each person for a few seconds. Be mindful that eye contact patterns are different for speaking and for listening – in the United States, listeners look more than speakers do. They also are different from culture to culture – for instance, the Japanese are generally less comfortable with extended eye contact than Americans. Other non-verbal signals are also important to the attitude we convey, though their interpretation and impact vary across cultures.

Nonverbal expressions of competence and warmth:

- Eye contact
- Hand gestures
- Head tilt
- Posture and distance

A second nonverbal technique to build the impression of competence and warmth is to keep your hands in front of your torso, elbows bent and palms up. This pose allows you to gesture easily when speaking to reinforce your words. Avoid pointing at people, which is considered aggressive and dominant in many cultures. Keeping your hands open rather than clutching an object, fiddling with objects, or tenting your fingers, looks relaxed and receptive.

Third, be aware of how you hold your head. Tilting it makes you seem attentive, especially when combined with eye contact. Nodding your head as you listen can encourage the other person to continue speaking. However, constant nodding looks habitual and can work against your intended impression. Be aware that some cultures interpret a nod to mean, "I agree," not just "I'm listening." In addition, there are gender differences in the use of this nonverbal behavior. In the United States women tilt and nod their heads more than men do while listening.

A fourth nonverbal technique is to maintain a posture that makes you look involved, alert, and open. Whether standing or sitting, keep your body relaxed, leaning slightly in as you listen and speak. The distance you are expected to maintain during conversations will vary from culture to culture. In the US business environment, "social distance" is typically three to five feet. Getting within arm's reach is considered "intimate"; it can also be interpreted as aggressive and asserting power or authority. On the other hand, staying apart five feet is considered "public," too formal for social interaction in small groups. Be sensitive to cultural preferences when seeking a comfortable distance.

Asking Questions

So far, we've examined two strategies for checking understanding – listening and reading nonverbals. A third strategy that will help you when you're trying to understand a message is to ask good questions. The type of answer you get will depend on the type of question you ask (see Table 4.1).

An *open-ended* question calls for a long answer. It is designed to open the door and get the other person talking. Typically it begins with "why," "what," "how," or "tell me about." You usually use open-ended questions at the beginning of a conversation.

A *closed-ended* question calls for a one-word answer such as a fact, a number, a date, a "yes" or "no." Typically it begins with "when," "how often," "how many," "will you," or "did you." You usually use closed-ended questions during a conversation to pin down information and at the end of a conversation to seek commitment.

A *probe* is a secondary or follow-up question. It can be open or closed. When you want the speaker to elaborate, ask an open probe such as "And

Table 4.1 Types of Questions

Question Type	Use	Example
Open	Get information	What happened?
	Get the other person talking	What are you worried about?
Closed	Get commitment	Will you do that?
	Get facts and details	When did that happen?
Probe	Get elaboration	What happened after that?
	Get clarification	Was that before or after he called?
Directed	Get agreement	That was a mistake, wasn't it?

then what did they do?" When you want the speaker to provide clarification, ask a closed probe such as "How often have they done that?"

A *directed* question is a leading question. Typically, it begins with a statement and then calls for agreement. An example is, "You won't be late for work again, will you?" Use a directed question toward the end of a conversation, when you are seeking consensus.

Listening to the Grapevine

Our discussion of listening has emphasized formal speaking/listening situations at work. However, informal, casual listening can also be extremely important. As a manager, you should always be aware of the rumors that circulate on the grapevine. At times, these rumors can provide important information; at other times, it may be important to change the rumors; and sometimes it's best to ignore the rumors. But always stay tuned in.

What causes rumors in contemporary workplaces? To answer this question, the following formula is helpful:

Rumors = Ambiguity × Interest

Rumors are created when the situation is ambiguous. If all information were available and clear from the formal channels, no rumors would be created. When the situation is ambiguous and also interesting, rumors will fly. This relationship has an important implication for managers. By paying attention to the grapevine, you can determine what is interesting to your employees.

Research indicates that information on an organization's grapevine is 70 to 90 percent accurate. However, some amount of distortion always exists.[xv] This core of truth along with the degree of distortion is often what makes a message on the grapevine believable, interesting, and durable.

As information moves from person to person on the grapevine, it tends to undergo three kinds of change. The first is *leveling,* where details are dropped or simplified. This process is especially prevalent when the rumor is extremely complex. The second kind of change is *sharpening,* where people add drama and vivid details. Employees work to make a story better and more entertaining as they pass it along. The third is *assimilating,* the tendency of people to adjust or modify rumors, to mold them to fit their personal needs. This makes the rumor more useful to those feeding the grapevine.[xvi]

If you are going to listen effectively to informal communication, you need to determine the extent to which leveling, sharpening, and assimilation have occurred. Inaccurate rumors can sometimes call for action. Let's say you work in a manufacturing environment, and rumors are flying about a massive layoff because of the new machinery being installed. If you hear these incorrect rumors, you shouldn't ignore them. Instead, members of the management team should meet formally with the opinion leaders among employees to assure them no layoffs will occur and the new equipment will offer significant benefits. Listening to rumors will help you to prevent losses in employee morale. As one manager once said to me, "It's important to listen to the talk on the street."

Employees prefer to get their information from formal channels, but they turn to informal channels when the formal ones have dried up because no one can work in a vacuum. Managers concerned about rampant rumors should keep in mind the relationship between formal and informal channels.

Summary

"Getting along" begins with knowing yourself and managing yourself. Once you have gained competency in self-awareness and self-management, you can become competent in social awareness and be able to manage relationships for maximum outcomes.

The goal is to stay informed about what's going on around you. To do that, you must nurture the communication channels between you and your direct reports, peers, and bosses. To check how well you understand what's going on, listen, read nonverbals, and ask questions. You can use the strategies presented in this chapter for keeping information flowing in formal and informal channels. An informed manager is a high-performing manager.

Notes

i Lucia Stretcher Sigmar, Geraldine E. Hynes, and Kathy L. Hill (2012). "Strategies for Teaching Social and Emotional Intelligence in Business Communication," *Business Communication Quarterly,* Vol. 75, no. 3, pp. 301–317.

   ii Travis Bradberry and Jean Greaves (2009). *Emotional Intelligence 2.0*. Talent Smart.

  iii David Ryback (2012). *Putting Emotional Intelligence to Work* (New York: Routledge).

  iv Bradberry and Greaves (2009). *Emotional Intelligence 2.0*.

   v Daniel Goleman (1995). *Emotional Intelligence* (New York, NY: Bantam Publishing Co.).

  vi B.A. Stipleman, E. Rice, A.L. Vogel, and K.L. Hall (2019). "Comprehensive Collaboration Plans: Practical Considerations Spanning Across Individual Collaborators to Institutional Supports," in Kara L. Hall, Amanda L. Vogel, & Robert T. Croyle (eds.), *Strategies for Team Science Success* (Springer) pp.587–611. DOI:10.1007/978-3-030-2 0992-6_45.

 vii A. Nadkarni, N. C. Levy-Carrick, D. S. Kroll, D. Gitlin, and D. Silbersweig (2021). "Communication and Transparency as a Means to Strengthening Workplace Culture During COVID-19," *NAM Perspectives*, National Academy of Medicine, Washington, DC. Retrieved from https://doi.org/10.31478/202103a

viii I.M. Sixel (2013, May 16). "Permission to Speak Freely to the Boss," *Houston Chronicle*, p. D1.

  ix Sixel.

   x William B. Gudykunst (1998). *Bridging Differences: Effective Intergroup Communication*, 3rd ed. (Thousand Oaks, CA: SAGE), pp. 173–174.

  xi Joel Whalen, (2022, March). "A Scientific Explanation for the Degree of Misunderstanding When Communicating," *Association for Business Communication Newsletter*. Unpublished.

 xii Mary Munter, (2012). *Guide to Managerial Communication: Effective Business Writing and Speaking*, 9th ed. Prentice Hall, p. 154.

xiii Julien C. Mirivel, Ryan Fuller, Amy Young, and Kristen Christman (2022, January 30). "Integrating Positive Communication Principles and Practices in Business Communication Courses," *The Western Association for Business Communication Bulletin*. Retrieved from https://abcwest.org/2022/01/30/integrating-positive-communication-principles-and-practices-in-business-communication-courses/

xiv Julia T. Wood (2013). *Gendered Lives: Communication, Gender, and Culture*, 10th ed. (Boston: Wadsworth), p. 127.

 xv Hugh B. Vickery (1984, January). "Tapping into the Employee Grapevine," *Association Management*, pp. 59–64.

xvi Philip V. Lewis (1987). *Organizational Communication: The Essence of Effective Management*, 3rd ed. (New York: Wiley & Sons), pp. 46–48.

Chapter 5

Strategies for Strengthening Work Relationships

"Getting along" on the job means developing and maintaining strong work relationships. In the previous chapter, we saw that relationships are built on communication – if there is no communication, there is no relationship. Think of someone you see around your worksite from time to time but you haven't ever talked with. Do you have a relationship with that person? No. Now think of someone at work that you do engage with – a boss, a direct report, or a peer. Do you have a relationship with that person? Yes, of course. Whether the relationship is negative or positive, whether you like or dislike that person, your relationship is the result of interpersonal communication.

Chapter 4 described a number of strategies for finding out what's going on in your work environment. These strategies for listening, checking understanding, and responding are invaluable communication competencies. As the Sequence for Success model (Figure 5.1) shows, interpersonal communication leads to interpersonal relationships.

Now that we have explored the connection between communication competence and interpersonal relationships, we are ready to move further up the Sequence for Success and explore the connection between interpersonal relationships and several other important elements – loyalty, commitment, job satisfaction, and trust. When those emotional conditions are present, people are more productive because they can work together more smoothly. In Part III of this book we will describe how "getting along" leads to "getting it done."

The New Golden Rule

As a child, you may have been taught to "do unto others as you would have them do unto you." This maxim is based on the ethic of reciprocity, and its roots can be traced back over four thousand years. Variations of the Golden Rule are found in writings from ancient Egypt, Greece, China, and other cultures, as well as most major religions of the world.

In the workplace, it makes some sense to treat others as you would like to be treated. However, as a manager, you need to do better. When building

DOI: 10.4324/9781003335177-7

© Geraldine E. Hynes

Figure 5.1 The Sequence for Success.

relationships, try treating others as *they* want to be treated, not the way *you* want to be treated. Sharon Sloane, CEO of Will Interactive, a maker of training videos, calls this version of the Golden Rule the "Platinum Rule: do unto others as they would have you do unto them."[i] She explains that this ethic recognizes that not everybody is motivated by the same thing that motivates you. In short, leaders should figure out what makes their people tick.

The Platinum Rule: Treat others as they want to be treated, not the way you want to be treated.

Managing by the Platinum Rule starts with using your communication competencies to learn about your people and what's going on with them, then building a relationship based on that knowledge. Briefly, the strategies introduced in Chapter 4 that will help you understand people at work are:

1 Observe their verbal and nonverbal behavior
2 Ask questions to test the accuracy of your observations
3 Walk in their shoes to gain understanding and empathy

Ask yourself, "If I were this person, how would I feel? What would I say? How would I react?" Developing empathy is particularly important – and difficult – in a culturally diverse workplace. However, conflict management, decision making, problem solving, and other leadership activities are much easier and more effective when "dynamic connectedness" among workers is present. Dynamic connectedness is a term widely used by economists when analyzing the impact of world events such as the COVID-19 pandemic on stock markets.[ii] The term is useful when describing how daily communication impacts interpersonal relations in the work environment. No longer do people work alone; 100 percent of the Fortune 500 companies and 90 percent of all US companies implement some form of group decision process. Teamwork demands strong interdependent relationships.

Empathy

Having close relationships with colleagues – even just one – makes a difference in personal and organizational growth. Bridges are built across cultural divides one person at a time. Researchers at the University of Chicago provide evidence for this claim. They studied hundreds of teenagers from cultures that are historically in conflict (Israelis and Palestinians, Catholics and Protestants in Northern Ireland, rural whites, and urban blacks in the United States). Since 1993 the Seeds of Peace program has brought teenagers together for a three-week summer camp in Maine, sleeping, eating, playing games, and participating in discussions. The University of Chicago researchers measured how the relationships that the students developed with each other during their camp experiences changed their attitudes.

The results are striking. Regardless of their initial attitudes, the teens who formed just one close relationship with someone from the other group were the ones who developed the most positive attitudes toward the other group. The conclusion is that forming just one friendship was as good or better a predictor of future attitudes toward the conflicting group than the total number of friendships that a person formed.[iii]

Creating opportunities for coworkers and subordinates to interact informally will foster empathy.

As a manager, you can foster the development of empathy among your employees by forming them into teams or workgroups and assigning them a project. The proximity and forced interaction will pave the way toward empathic relationships. That's because the group members will have to find common ground. Further, as the employees engage with each other, they will become more emotionally invested in the organization. Ultimately, the organization will become smarter and more effective because the work of organizations is done through person-to-person relationships.

These strategies apply to horizontal as well as vertical work relationships. Just as you can influence your direct reports to develop empathy, there are ways to encourage empathy among your peers. For instance, you can gather everyone to celebrate an achievement, a holiday, or even a birthday. That will give people an opportunity to exchange perceptions and learn about each other in a low-stress environment. Informal, face-to-face interactions work best for developing empathy because both verbal and nonverbal cues are exchanged; the combination gives a more complete understanding of the information being shared.

"Lean" communication channels such as virtual meetings, text messages, and email exchanges are a poor substitute for face-to-face interactions. If your associates are scattered in the field or telecommuting from remote locations, it's more difficult for them to develop empathic relationships. Be creative. For instance, you can mimic watercooler chat opportunities by beginning your Zoom meetings with an exercise like this one, recommended by Jerod Venema, CEO of Liveswitch, Inc.: each team member takes a turn sharing a personal win along with a work win. Not only does everyone get a peek into others' non-work lives, but they also discover work-related achievements.

Loyalty, Commitment, and Job Satisfaction

A study by the Great Place to Work Institute found that employees enjoy working where they "trust the people they work for, have pride in what they do, and enjoy the people they work with."[iv] Open, two-way communication is a hallmark of such workplaces.

Loyalty and commitment to an organization increase when employees "feel a strong emotional bond to their employer, recommending it to others and committing time and effort to help the organization succeed."[v] Committed employees have been linked to important organizational outcomes such as higher retention, fewer safety violations, reduced absenteeism, and perhaps most importantly, higher productivity.[vi]

Managerial communication has consistently been identified as a key factor in employee commitment. As discussed in Chapter 4, honest, frequent communication keeps workers informed about the organization's goals and how they can contribute to reaching the goals. One company I consulted with found that the need for periodic employee meetings with the CEO became unnecessary when they built communication into the culture of their organization. As routine communication improved, attendance at the meetings with the CEO dwindled to nothing. "We already know what is going on" was the employees' explanation.

An additional benefit of consistent, honest, and frequent communication is that it makes workers feel appreciated and respected. When employees believe you support them, they respond by becoming more committed and engaged in their job. Engaged employees have a strong, positive relationship with their manager. Putting it another way, employees don't quit their job, they quit their boss.

Employees don't quit their job, they quit their boss.

Employee engagement has become a major theme in current management literature. In a recent Gallup poll, a startling 70 percent of American workers said they were not engaged with their jobs or were actively disengaged. When asked why, the workers complained about the lack of opportunity for self-expression, personal growth, and meaningful work. Finding meaning is about being engaged. It's about feeling important, feeling recognized, and feeling informed.

Employee engagement levels are down all across the United States, but they appear to be particularly weak among Millennials. In a Harris Interactive report commissioned by the Career Advisory Board, "meaning" was the top career priority for those between the ages of 21 and 31. If you are from a previous generation, like me, you are more likely to value loyalty to the company above meaningful work. You may even be willing to admit that you've complained about younger employees' lack of commitment to their organization. But it's risky for managers to ignore such generational differences in priorities, whether real or imagined, because they may affect morale, retention, and even productivity.

The single best tool to enhance engagement is face-to-face, one-to-one communication. You can increase your employees' level of engagement by making small but key changes in your daily workplace interactions. You can talk to your people more often than emailing them. You can notice their contributions more often than their mistakes. You can simply ask your employees whether they had a good day and what moments made it so.[vii] Then listen. Try to adjust the work environment to make those moments happen more frequently.

Mirivel (2014) introduced a model of positive communication that is grounded in six communicative behaviors and principles."[viii] The behaviors are (1) greeting, (2) asking, (3) complimenting, (4) disclosing, (5) encouraging, and (6) listening (Table 5.1). First, greetings can help you to acknowledge others, open a sequence of communication between two or more people, and serve to both affirm and identify the nature of your relationship with others and your status. Second, you can place yourself in a position to discover others. Shift the script of your interactions by, for instance, asking open questions rather than closed questions. Third, you can

Table 5.1 Mirivel's Positive Communication Behaviors

Behavior	Function	Examples
Greet	Create contact	Greet coworkers warmly each day. Initiate a bit of small talk with each coworker. Reach out to employees working remotely.
Ask	Discover the unknown	Avoid closed questions ("Do you have any questions?" "Is this clear?" "Are you following me?") Ask more open questions ("What is confusing?" "How can I help you?")
Compliment	Affect the sense of self	Provide affirming feedback that is actionable and sincere. Use the **BET** formula: identify a concrete, specific **B**ehavior. Explain the **E**ffect of the behavior. **T**hank the recipient.
Disclose	Deepen relationships	Talk about hobbies and outside interests that makes you more relatable. Disclose your own struggles and challenges relevant to the work. Share stories of your career path to help others.
Encourage	Give support	Send notes of encouragement during stressful times to let employees know you are thinking about them. Express confidence in the success of the project.
Listen	Transcend differences	Paraphrase to check understanding. Use the **HSR** formula to build commonality without trying to fix the problem: **H**eard, **S**een, **R**espected.

compliment people, thereby strengthening their sense of self and building people up. Fourth, you can be more vulnerable, transparent, and honest in your communication to strengthen connections at work. Fifth, you can encourage and give social support that inspires, instills confidence, and helps others to actualize. Sixth, you can listen deeply to others to minimize perceived differences. Managers who are perceived as good listeners positively impact employees' job satisfaction and even reduce turnover. [ix]

Here's another strategy to boost engagement: a retention survey. To keep your workers from going elsewhere, find out why they are unhappy. To keep your workers happy, find out why they stay. Conducting an exit survey may reveal the working conditions – or people – that drove someone away, but it's too late at that point to impact the leaver's attitudes. Instead, conduct a retention survey among current employees. A retention survey can make people feel valued and will determine what the company can do to improve employee satisfaction, whether it's training, benefits, improved communication channels, or recognition programs. Sometimes you can reassign or even redesign the individual's job to make it more closely align with personal strengths and passions.

> An engaged workforce is a happier workforce and a more productive workforce.

For maximum impact, responsibility for employee engagement should be corporate-wide. Indeed, in the best companies, a culture of open communication begins with the CEO and other top executives, who know that employees must be engaged so they will contribute to the company's goals. Internal communication processes are in place in these companies to ensure that employees understand the company's mission and how they fit into it.

Companies with an open communication culture invest in a range of platforms to support employee dialog and promote engagement. Meetings, webcasts, executive presentations, newsletters, feedback mechanisms, forums, company blogs, and other interactive media are examples of formal internal channels designed to build engagement. As a vice president of an energy company said, "The more employees understand and feel like they're contributing or in line with the company strategy, the more productive they are and the higher the morale and [the] lower [the] turnover."[x]

Trust

Putting your employees first, helping them to feel engaged and committed, is a matter of trust above all else. Employees who are not engaged in what they do, don't trust their managers or their companies. Today's employees are looking for a place where they can do their best work. They are looking for cultural fit and trusting relationships on the job.

Trusting Them

If you want your employees to trust you, then you must trust them. Remember Sharon Sloane, CEO of Will Interactive? Here's the extent to which she trusts her people:

> "We give what we call mission-type orders here. I will be very clear with what the goal is, what the objective is. Then I'm basically going to give you the latitude to do it. If you need my help or have a problem, come see me. Otherwise, I bless you."[xi]

Trusting your employees means nurturing their independence, allowing workers freedom to express their opinions and follow preferred work styles without denying those of others. This willingness to let people approach the work their preferred way – so long as the goal is achieved – is particularly important if you have a culturally diverse workforce. Diverse environments call for a high tolerance for disagreement. Ask yourself, "Which is more important – that things get done my way, or that things get done?"

A healthy work climate is a trusting climate. Douglas McGregor, an expert in organizational communication, summarized the optimal characteristics of a work climate:

1   The atmosphere is informal, relaxed, and comfortable.
2   Everyone participates in discussions about the work at hand.
3   Everyone is committed to the task and the objective.
4   Everyone listens to each other. Every idea is given a fair hearing.
5   Disagreement is not suppressed. Rather than silencing dissent, the reasons are examined, and the group seeks rational solutions.
6   Important decisions are reached by consensus.
7   Criticism is frequent, frank, and relatively comfortable, but not personal.
8   People freely express their feelings.
9   The leader does not dominate.
10 The group monitors itself.[xii]

Do these characteristics sound like the characteristics of your work group? If you are comfortable hearing differences expressed, if you trust people to find their own way to reach the performance goal, the result will be relational satisfaction, commitment to excellence, and organizational success.

Trusting You

Of course, if you want your employees to trust you, you need to be trustworthy, yourself. The following paragraphs present ways to develop trust. Briefly, trust is developed when

1   your words are consistent with your nonverbals and actions
2   your behaviors are predictable
3   you explain what is going on and why (transparency)

Elements of trust:

- Consistency
- Predictability
- Transparency

Let's take a closer look at these factors. First, make your words, nonverbals, and actions consistent. As you read in Chapter 4, when what you say is inconsistent with how you look and sound, people believe how you look and sound. For instance, if you say, "These procedural changes are going to be an improvement," while looking glum, your people won't believe the changes will be beneficial, and they will resist adopting them.

Appropriate nonverbal behaviors for managers can be summarized as those demonstrating a confident manner. Confidence builds trust. Stand and sit straight, keep your head balanced on your neck, and be aware of eye contact patterns. Use a clear, pleasant but strong tone of voice and minimize disfluencies ("uh," "um," "you know," "like").

Appropriate verbal behaviors for managers who want to build trust include using inclusive words to indicate that both you and your listeners belong to a group. Words such as "we," "us," and "our" rather than "I" and "my" signal a social category that will increase loyalty and trust for members of the in-group. Another verbal tool is to disclose more frequently, sharing information as much and as often as you can. This will reduce uncertainty and increase trust, even if people won't like what they hear. Telling them more about what's going on will also increase predictability. A third verbal tool is to use concrete language – facts and words with clear meanings – rather than abstract or vague terms. Speaking conceptually or with lofty, vague expressions causes doubt and distrust.

Trustworthy talk is

- Inclusive
- Frequent
- Complete
- Concrete

Finally, trustworthy talk is honest. The 2012 Edelman Trust Barometer calls for companies to "practice radical transparency," which means telling employees the truth about what's going on.[xiii] If a company shares information, employees feel a sense of belonging and a part of a shared mission. This develops a bond of trust between employees and the company. Leaders who are transparent, who openly share truthful information with their workers, retain credibility.

Diversity and Work Relationships

Diversity has been found to increase team productivity and the quality of work. Diversity includes factors such as gender, ethnicity, religious beliefs, career stage, personality, socioeconomic class, life experiences, viewpoints, and time management. Perhaps most importantly, diversity applies to the ways people think about and solve problems.

Culturally sensitive managers are aware that these factors influence team interactions and can be a source of conflict. One strategy that you can use to build your heterogeneous team's interpersonal skills and appreciation for DEIA is teamwork exercises. Employees may be unexcited about participating in such exercises, especially when they are conducted outside the workplace, but they have important benefits. Try beginning with simple changes like the seating arrangement during meetings so members get to know one another, become attuned to similarities and differences in points of view, and generally stimulate emotional engagement. More ideas for designing and delivering communication training are presented in Chapter 6.

You also can conduct assessment exercises to help your teams establish norms (explicit standards for behavior) and measure their progress toward goals. Periodic assessments can take various forms and can be formal or informal, so long as everyone gets to voice their opinions. The ultimate value of teamwork training and assessment is that they foster a culture that values and promotes collaboration.[xiv]

Let's take a closer look at one aspect of diversity that often influences multicultural teams. So far, this chapter has focused on how to strengthen work relationships in a democratic, egalitarian culture. However, today's workplace requires recognizing that there are significant differences in what people of other cultures think are appropriate relationships among workers in hierarchical organizations.

Cultures that value authoritarian leadership reward managers who are directive, prescriptive, and judgmental. The boss's word is not to be questioned. Employees are expected to be dependent and submissive, suppressing their opinions. An example of such a culture is Korea. In his best-selling book, *Outliers*, Malcolm Gladwell described Korean national airlines as once having the worst accident record of all. Careful investigation of the reasons for the alarming frequency of plane crashes revealed that they were often due to pilot error. Apparently, even when crew members perceived their captain making mistakes, they didn't try to correct the captain, because they believed it was not their place to question authority. Once training programs incorporated the notion that calling attention to potential errors was a crew-member's duty, the airline's record of accidents improved significantly.

In authoritarian cultures where leaders are expected to be dominant (and some US companies are still like that), the strategies emphasized in this chapter will fail, and managers who apply them will be considered weak. For example, some companies in Spain and Portugal are more likely to emphasize the importance of interpersonal communication and employee satisfaction than companies in Germany and France.

To become a culturally sensitive manager, you need to assess your employees' personal achievement needs and relationship expectations and create a work environment that maximizes everyone's comfort level. If you're not sure about the implications of what you are observing, ask questions. The goal is to gain communication competence across contexts.

Summary

Getting along at work involves building and maintaining relationships. This chapter presents communication strategies designed to strengthen relationships among workers and also between workers and their managers so they can "get along." First, the new Golden Rule is to treat others as they want to be treated. Foster dynamic connectedness by creating opportunities for formal and informal get-togethers so workers can form empathic relationships.

Loyalty, commitment, and job satisfaction will grow when employees feel engaged in meaningful work. Trust will develop when managers are consistent and predictable in their verbal and nonverbal behavior. Communication that is frequent, true, and comprehensive will also contribute to trustworthiness.

Managers of high-performing work teams can foster appreciation for DEIA with periodic team exercises and assessments. The outcomes include improved communication, agreement on norms, collaboration, and productivity.

Notes

i Adam Bryant (2014, August 3). "See Yourself as Others See You: Interview with Sharon Sloane." *The New York Times*, p. 2.

ii Manel Youssef, Khaled Mokni, and Ahdi Noomen Ajmi (2021). "Dynamic Connectedness Between Stock Markets in the Presence of the COVID-19 Pandemic: Does Economic Policy Uncertainty Matter?" *Financial Innovation*, ISSN 2199–4730, Springer, Heidelberg, Vol. 7, no. 1, pp. 1–27, https://doi.org/10.1186/s40854-021-00227-3.

iii Juliana Schroeder and Jane L. Risen (2014, July 28). 'Befriending The Enemy: Outgroup Friendship Longitudinally Predicts Intergroup Attitudes In A Coexistence Program For Israelis And Palestinians." *Group Processes and Intergroup Relations Journal*. DOI: 10.1177/1368430214542257.

iv A. B. Carroll (2006, July 29). "Trust Is The Key When Rating Great Workplaces." Retrieved from http://onlineathens.com/stories/073006/business_20060730047.shtml, p. 1.

v B. Quirk (2008). *Making the Connections: Using Internal Communication To Turn Strategy Into Action* (Burlington, VT: Gower), p. 102.

vi J. Robison (2012, January 5). "Boosting Engagement at Stryker". *Gallup Management Journal*. Retrieved from http://gmj.gallup.com/content/150956/Boosting-Engagement-Stryker.aspx. p. 1.

vii Aaron Hurst (2014, April 20). "Being 'Good' Isn't the Only Way to Go." *Houston Chronicle*, p. B2.

viii J.C. Mirivel (2014). *The Art of Positive Communication: Theory and Practice* (New York: Peter Lang Publishing), p. 7.

ix A. Bregenzer, B. Milfelner, S. Šarotar Žižek, and P. Jiménez (2020). "Health-Promoting Leadership And Leaders' Listening Skills Have An Impact On The Employees' Job Satisfaction And Turnover Intention." *International Journal of Business Communication*, 2329488420963700.

x Karen Mishra, Lois Boynton, and Aneil Mishra (2014). "Driving Employee Engagement: The Expanded Role of Internal Communications." *International Journal of Business Communication*, Vol. 51, no. 2, p. 191.

xi Adam Bryant.

xii Douglas McGregor (1960). *The Human Side of Enterprise* (New York: McGraw-Hill).

xiii Edelman Trust Barometer (2012). *Executive summary*. Retrieved from http://www.scribd.com/doc/79026497/2012-Edelman-Trust-Barometer-Executive-Summary.

xiv Kendra S Cheruvelil, Patricia A Soranno, Kathleen C Weathers, Paul C Hanson, Simon J Goring, Christopher T Filstrup, and Emily K Read (2014). "Creating and Maintaining High-Performing Collaborative Research Teams: The Importance of Diversity And Interpersonal Skills." *Frontiers in Ecology and the Environment*, Vol. 12, no. 1, pp. 31–38. DOI: 10.1890/130001.

Part III

Get It Done

Chapter 6

Strategies for Communicating Job Expectations

So far in this book we've looked at strategies that will help you to "get along" at work. We've described communication techniques you can use to find out what's going on around you and to strengthen your work relationships. Networking is an invaluable survival skill in today's diverse workplace. And building an open, trusting environment allows employees to perform at their peak.

After you've learned how to get along with others on the job, you need to find ways to "get it done," which is the theme of this section. It's all about the daily workplace interaction skills that you as a manager need to use in order to keep your people motivated and productive. Wouldn't your job be simple if people did what they were supposed to do and thought that their paychecks were sufficient reward? But a manager's work isn't simple, because every day you are dealing with human nature.

This section on how to "get it done" includes four chapters. This chapter gives you strategies for making sure your employees understand what they are expected to do on the job. Chapter 7 explains how to give performance feedback, both positive and corrective. Continuing our examination of tough communication challenges that you face every day, Chapter 8 discusses workplace conflict and offers five strategies for managing it. Chapter 9 focuses on another communication challenge – figuring out when someone is being dishonest with you.

Communicating Job Expectations

If you've ever been surprised and disappointed when an employee said, "I don't know how to do that" or "I didn't know you wanted me to do that," this chapter is for you. Just because a new hire supposedly has the job qualifications a position requires, that doesn't guarantee that he can hit the ground running. Rather than assuming he will step right in, it's important to take the time to communicate your expectations as clearly and completely as you can. That will not only reduce the employee's performance anxiety, but it will also build a trusting relationship. It will also minimize

DOI: 10.4324/9781003335177-9

the frequency that you will need the skills described in Chapter 7, how to give corrective feedback.

The Tell-Show-Do Formula

The classic model for teaching new employees how to do a job is "Tell-Show-Do." I stumbled on this model when I was 18 years old and a freshman in college. I had been working part-time as a file clerk at the Credit Bureau of Cook County, Illinois, for the previous two years. When my supervisor heard that I had recently graduated from high school and was now in college, she decided that my new educational status qualified me to become the trainer on the night shift. Figure 6.1 shows the training model I followed, which builds on the original three-step formula.

Back then, credit records consisted of envelopes with pieces of paper in them that detailed car loan terms, department store credit card activity, home mortgages, liens, collections, and the like. The envelopes were filed in enormous metal cabinets in an enormous building in downtown Chicago. Yes, it's true – this was during the pre-computer era. For security reasons, a fairly sophisticated coding system was used for organizing the files rather than in alphabetical order. My assignment was to train the newly hired nightshift clerks on the coding system so they could find files and report the information in them to our clients.

Tell

I first found some codebooks, made copies, and laminated them. I called them cheat sheets, though I later learned the term, "job aids." Each class began with me going through the cheat sheets with the trainees, telling

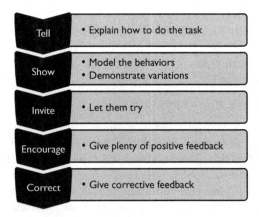

Figure 6.1 Training Model.

them how to decode existing file contents and how to code new information. I quizzed them on the codes as we went along, to hasten their memorization. I told them about the rules, procedures, and policies that governed the work they would be expected to do.

Show

Next I wheeled a basket of credit files into the training room, picked one file out of the basket at random, opened it, showed the trainees what was inside, and helped them to understand what each number and piece of paper meant. They watched as I handled the material, filing and refiling it properly, explaining variations. The basic idea behind this step was to demonstrate examples of the work they would be expected to perform, and "non-examples" of mistakes to avoid.

Do

During our last class, I gave each trainee a basket of files and invited them to go through it themselves, figuring out what it contained and why the information was organized the way it was. They worked in teams while I stood by, guiding and answering questions that their teammates couldn't. On "graduation night," the trainees returned to the main floor, and I shadowed them as they applied their new skills in the actual work environment, coaching them along and handling problems. I found that positive feedback, called **Encourage** in Figure 6.1, was a powerful motivator. Of course, tactful negative feedback, called **Correct** in Figure 6.1, was sometimes necessary.

You may be interested to know that the Tell-Show-Do method was pioneered by an American educational psychologist named Robert Gagne, who had worked with the Army Air Corps during World War II to train pilots. After the war, he spent the rest of his career perfecting and testing his instructional design model, first publishing it in 1965 as the "Nine Events of Instruction."[i] Since then, extensive research has validated Gagne's principles in educational settings, though I know from first-hand experience that the principles also apply to work settings.[ii]

Formal Training Programs

If you expect your employees to do certain tasks and they aren't doing them correctly, don't jump to conclusions about their motivations, work attitudes, or intellect. First, check to be sure that they understand what you want them to do. The following paragraphs will provide an overview of the training cycle, taking you through the process of determining what employees know and don't know, designing and delivering formal training, and conducting follow-up evaluations.

Steps in the Training Cycle:

1   Conduct a needs assessment
2   Design instructional materials
3   Determine logistics
4   Help adults learn
5   Evaluate outcomes

1. Conduct a Needs Assessment

The most obvious way to determine what employees already know and doesn't know is to ask. But if you say, "Do you know how to do this?" they will usually say, "Yes, I do" out of fear that they will look incompetent.

Instead, try an open-ended question like, "Tell me (or show me) how you do this." The gap between what they are doing and what you want them to do is the need for training. The traditional goal of training is to close that gap between actual and optimal behaviors.

Optimal behavior – Actual behavior = Training Need

I will pause here to say that the training needs assessment process not only determines important deviations from a standard. Managers can also use the TNA process to anticipate changes in standards and prepare employees to meet them. Thus, needs assessment can be proactive as well as reactive. Similarly, employees' learning needs can be considered as an opportunity as well as a problem. In short, training facilitates change. This approach reflects the fact that the concept of "the job" is becoming irrelevant today. Organizations have introduced broadbanding, multiskilling, and career path planning into previously static occupations. Skill requirements quickly change to meet new market demands and new social and economic imperatives. Training is seen as part of an organic learning experience rather than a didactic process. The goal, rather than teaching learners what they do not know, is to build on what is already known.

Thus, the proactive approach actively seeks out ways to help people further develop strengths and encourages them to improve the quality of their contribution to the organization. The trainer's role is to prepare people with the skills to cope with ever-changing requirements. Training is defined as facilitating change.

Of course, you can't solve every performance problem or prepare for every organizational need through training. Maybe there's an absence of *incentive*; that is, the employees see no consequences of their behavior, no feedback, rewards, or punishments. Maybe there's an absence of *environmental support*; that is, the employees have inadequate or wrong tools, resources, staff, formal policies and procedures, or space. Maybe there's a lack of *motivation*; that is, the employees don't believe in or value the behavior, product, or process you expect them to follow.

These are just a few factors that you should consider when analyzing employee performance. But if your analysis shows that the employees need training, the second step is to design an instructional program.

2. Design Instructional Materials

Remember my story about training at the Credit Bureau of Cook County? Putting yourself in the shoes of the new hires, which do you think was more effective – reading the codebooks, listening to my explanations, watching my demonstrations?

Extensive research shows that most people are visual learners. That is, they remember what they see better than what they read or hear. In fact, listening is one of the poorest ways to learn for most people.

As Figure 6.2 shows, if your employees just listen, they will lose 90 percent of what you say after three days.[iii] For maximum retention, you need to appeal to a combination of senses – give them something to look at, something to listen to, and something to read.

In summary, instructional materials should appeal to a range of senses – sight, touch, sound, even taste – and involve a range of activities. Dreary lectures don't work well. The rule of training is to change things up every 20 minutes.

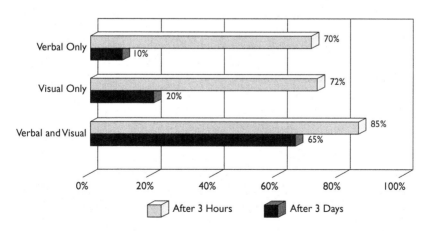

Figure 6.2 Percent of Audience Recall.

3. Determine Logistics

Once you have determined the need for training and put together some materials, you must figure out when, where, and how the training will be delivered. If employees are called off the job site so they can attend training, who will take their place, allowing the workflow to continue? What about the costs? Can vestibule training be used for a portion of the training? What about job shadowing? Managers should consider the pros and cons of a variety of delivery modes. Logistical issues can be daunting, so let's take a closer look at the two most often used training delivery modes.

Online delivery is a practical training mode that overcomes many logistical barriers. Web-based programs are popular because they can be efficient and cost-effective. Typically, employees work through the training package online at their own pace, and sometimes during their own time. Built-in measures of progress along the way can ensure that they don't just click through the material. Evidence of completion and test scores can be automatically reported back to the work unit and the People Operations Department.

Face-to-face training classes, by comparison, are more time-consuming and often more costly because of trainees' time away from work. Sessions are intensive but often more effective in terms of actual learning and facilitating behavior changes.

When choosing a delivery mode, consider the training topic. For instance, a new-hire orientation might lend itself best to vestibule training, while sexual harassment training may be better for web-based training. Other important considerations are the audience and the training budget. Oakwood Worldwide provides an example. A provider of temporary housing, Oakwood won the Top 125 Training Award for its training and development programs. It offers face-to-face and online classes for all associates and constantly adds to its course catalog. This is a major recruitment as well as a retention tool for its employees. In fact, the company credits this program for retaining 25 percent of its workforce for ten years or more.[iv]

Outside trainers are sometimes brought in, rather than using in-house trainers and managers, because they can provide a fresh, unbiased viewpoint and can offer a threat-free resource.

After deciding on the delivery format you will have to select a training source. Often, your People Operations Leader will help you find a vendor, either internal or external. Customized training is usually more costly than "off-the-shelf" prepackaged programs, but in the end it can be more effective because it is aimed at a narrower target of training needs.

Another logistical issue is who should attend. One consulting client made it mandatory for everyone from the receptionist to the president to come to communication training. At the same time. In one big room. You can imagine the uncomfortable silences when I brought up certain topics.

Another client, a law firm, hired me to conduct a teambuilding workshop with the firm's office assistants in an attempt to improve communication between the attorneys and their admins. When I suggested that the attorneys would benefit from attending the sessions, too, they balked. To convince the attorneys, I compared it to marriage counseling with just one spouse. Interestingly, the attorneys who did find time to show up had the fewest communication breakdowns with their staff.

A final, and crucial, logistical consideration is the content of the training program. Deciding what to cover usually requires that you develop *learning objectives* or goals – what you want the trainees to know and be able to do, explain, or demonstrate at the end of the training. Good learning objectives are performance-based, observable, and measurable. Here are some examples of learning objectives:

- Be able to explain the company policy on sexual harassment and give examples of sexual harassment.
- Be able to show the proper way to take a customer's order.
- Be able to use the new expense-tracking software.
- Be able to explain the safety procedure for handling chemicals.

Once your learning objectives are nailed down, you can compose a brief outline of the major topics to be covered. With that outline, you can "fill in" the major topics with information. Based on this information, you can develop modules and training materials such as PowerPoint slides, discussion topics, and job aids. Be sure to build in some evaluation tools as you go along.

4. Help Adults Learn

Logistical issues are complex. Often you have to make do with an imperfect schedule, compromising on content, time, place, and length. There may even be some controversy about snacks. But once you've nailed down all those decisions, you can move on to considering how adults learn best.

An effective face-to-face training class is organized as shown in Table 6.1. Notice the level of trainee involvement in each segment. Adults learn best when they see the value of the learning. So in order for them to buy into the training, they must be able to connect the information with their own goals. They should be actively engaged every step of the way.

Research on how adults learn indicates that there are four learning styles, as identified in Figure 6.3: personal, analytical, practical, and innovative.[v] Becoming aware of the diversity of learning styles will make you a more culturally competent manager and help you decide how to conduct the training.

Table 6.1 Organization of a Face-to-face Training Session

When	What
Beginning	• Set goals • Describe appropriate behaviors • Explain methods • Motivate participants to learn
Middle	• Broadcast structure of the program • Balance lecture, discussion, practice, Q & A sessions • Make learning fun, not frightening
End	• Review achievements • Discuss transfer of learning to the work environment • Suggest ways to reinforce the learning and overcome roadblocks • Give rewards

In the next paragraphs, we examine these four adult learning styles and their corresponding communication styles. Then we suggest training techniques to suit each.

The *Personal Learner* is high on feeling and watching. This style relates material to their personal experience and uses an *amiable* communication style, avoiding conflict. They learn well in groups, often being responsive and indirect so as to maintain relationships.

The *Analytical Learner* is high on thinking and watching. Their communication style is also *analytical*, needing structured environments and seeking to know how facts relate to established knowledge. They learn well from lectures and case studies.

The *Practical Learner* is high on doing and thinking. This style is assertive and results–oriented. They have a *driver* communication style and are comfortable sharing opinions and influencing others. They learn well from hands–on activities and simulations.

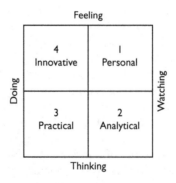

Figure 6.3 Learning Styles.

The *Innovative Learner* is high on doing and feeling. This style resists structure and enjoys considering possibilities. They have an *expressive* communication style, looking at things from all sides. They learn well from brainstorming exercises and experiments.

Take the time to identify your employees' preferred learning styles and communication styles. Then you will be able to develop training materials to suit them. Realize, however, that while it's not always practical or even possible, the best solution is to find a balance between nurturing and challenging (Figure 6.4). That is, try to build some elements into the training program that will maximize each learning style and communication style. For example, you could incorporate a group discussion for the personal learners, a brainstorming activity for the innovative learners, a case study for the analytical learners, and a simulation for the practical learners.

A training program that attempts to close the gap between actual and optimal behaviors, that is delivered in an efficient yet effective format, and that incorporates techniques designed to facilitate every learning style and communication style is likely to be successful.

5. Evaluate Outcomes

After your employees have received training, how can you be sure that it will stick? Donald Kirkpatrick, a top researcher in corporate training and development, identified four levels of evaluation and suggested that there are numerous ways to determine success.[vi]

The first level of evaluation is the trainees' *reaction*. Immediately post-program, ask the trainees how they liked the training. Usually you can accomplish this with a satisfaction survey that asks for ratings of the instructor, the materials, the logistics, and the topics. Such a survey is generally referred to as a "smile sheet." Typically, comments are limited to sweeping statements like, "the instructor was very lively," "I learned a lot," and "The room was too cold."

The second level of evaluation is trainee *learning*. Usually you can accomplish this with a test that you administer immediately post-program or

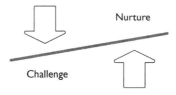

Figure 6.4 Balancing Act for Facilitating Learning.

after a short time has passed. Scores will indicate how much the trainees actually learned and remembered. You might need to design some re-inforcement tools that will remind them of what they learned every few weeks or months.

The third level of evaluation is trainee *behavior*. This is often the most important to managers because it measures whether the trainees can apply the new information back on the job. In most organizations, transfer of training is the bottom line when it comes to successful learning. Researchers at Purdue University reviewed 37 studies conducted over 30 years to determine what factors influence training transfer. The studies they reviewed considered such factors as trainees' individual characteristics, the work environment, and training program design. Yet, the most significant factor identified in the studies was the trainees' attitudes. That is, the more trainees are satisfied with their occupations and with the training, the more they will be motivated to transfer, the more they will learn, and the more frequently they will apply their newly acquired behaviors.[vii] So if transfer of training does not occur, look for barriers other than the trainee's ability. You may identify attitudinal and even environmental barriers to changing their behaviors.

The fourth level of evaluation is *results*. You can usually leave this level of evaluation to C-suite executives who have access to data about your work unit's productivity and performance pre- and post-training. Identifying the elements that affect return on investment (ROI) can be slippery since many factors other than employee competence will influence company performance.

Kirkpatrick's Levels of Training Evaluation:

1   Reaction
2   Learning
3   Behavior
4   Results

Let's examine a case to see how training evaluation can be applied to solve a business problem.

The Case of the Unused Equipment

Memorial Hospitals Group purchased new intravenous feeding equipment because it is more comfortable, safer, cleaner, and precisely controllable. Approximately 1/3 of the total units are currently in place in the hospitals, but few of them are being used. The new equipment comes with

Table 6.2 What Causes Performance Discrepancies at Memorial Hospitals Group?

Possible Cause	Questions to Ask
Skill/Knowledge	Does the IV work?
	Does staff know how to set up and maintain the IV?
	Is it a tougher process than the former IV?
Incentive	What happens if they use it? If they don't?
	How do supervisors respond to it?
Environment	Is the IV there? Where it's supposed to be?
	Is the old IV equally accessible?
Motivation	Does the staff know why the IV has appeared?
	Does the staff believe they can master the new IV?

information on how to maintain and use it. Still, staff avoids the new and relies on the old. Prior to purchasing thousands of additional IV units, management wants to make sure that the new ones are as good as promised. They can't check them out or provide better service to patients if the staff avoids the new equipment. In attempting to determine why the staff resist switching to the new IV equipment and whether training is the solution, they asked questions (see Table 6.2).

This case demonstrates that employee knowledge and skills may be just one of many factors affecting workplace behavior. Furthermore, the training aimed at closing the perceived gap between optimal and actual behavior might fail simply because the training was not the cause of the problem in the first place. Solid evaluation methods will reveal reasons for training success and failure.

Benefits of the Proactive Training Model

When evaluating training outcomes, so far we've considered four levels: employees' reactions, learning, behavior changes, and results. Thus, training evaluation has focused on activities that directly enhance the achievement of organizational goals. The training has leverage in that it contributes to specific activities.

As a final thought, be aware that there are also political payoffs for making the effort to develop your people. For one, such activities increase your visibility in the organization. When upper management is informed about the effectiveness of your training programs, they might come to perceive you as a resource for organization-wide development opportunities. People with this skill set are especially valued by "Learning Organizations." Furthermore, you gain credibility from your training activities. They demonstrate your functional area's expertise and reliability, putting it into the corporate mainstream. Visibility, credibility, centrality,

. and competence are benefits that could be significant for your professional future.

Summary

This chapter has provided guidelines for communicating performance expectations to your employees. To determine whether your direct reports understand what you want them to do, you can simply ask the question. If the answer is "no," the next step is to help them learn the expected tasks. You can explain by following the "tell-show-do" approach. When more formal instruction is called for, you can design, develop, and deliver a training program. You can help assure successful performance outcomes by effectively applying the five steps in the training process: assessing needs, developing instructional materials, making logistical arrangements, facilitating adult learning styles, and evaluating outcomes.

Notes

i Robert Gagne, *Nine Events of Instruction*. http://www.instructionaldesign.org/theories/conditions-learning.html

ii Joel L. Garner (2011). "How Award-winning Professors in Higher Education Use Merrill's First Principles of Instruction," *International Journal of Instructional Technology and Distance Learning*, Vol. 8, no. 5, pp. 3–16. See also Merrill, M. D. (2002). "First principles of instruction," *Educational Technology Research and Development*, Vol. 50, no. 3, pp. 43–59. For discussion of adaptations of the original three-step model, see also S.A. Beebe, T.P. Mottet, & K.D. Roach (2012). *Training and Development: Communicating for Success,* 2nd ed. (New York: Pearson).

iii Cheryl Hamilton (2013). *Communicating for Results: A Guide for Business and the Professions*, 10th ed. (New York: Cengage).

iv "Oakwood Worldwide Honored by Training Magazine for Fifth Consecutive Year: Training also Presents Oakwood with Best Practice Award," (2011, February 25). *Marketwire*, Retrieved from http://www.live-pr.com/en/oakwood-worldwide-honored-by-training-magazine-r1048761409.htm.

v David Kolb, and R. Fry (1975). "Toward an Applied Theory of Experiential Learning," in C. Cooper (ed.), *Theories of Group Process* (London: John Wiley). See also http://learningfromexperience.com

vi Donald Kirkpatrick and J.D. Kirkpatrick (2007). *Implementing the Four Levels* (Berrett-Koehler Publishers).

vii Mohan Yang and S. L. Watson (2021). "Attitudinal Influences on Transfer of Training: A Systematic Literature Review," *Performance Improvement Quarterly*, Vol. 34, no. 4, pp. 327–365. DOI: 10.1002/piq.

Chapter 7

Strategies for Giving Performance Feedback

The previous chapter presented strategies for explaining your performance expectations to the workgroup. After communicating job responsibilities, managers need to give feedback to employees about how well they are doing the job. This chapter offers strategies for informal corrective feedback and for maximizing the value of formal performance review interviews. It concludes by showing you how to develop an open communication climate in diverse environments that will support continued performance improvement.

Informal Performance Feedback

Whenever you notice an employee performing beyond expectations, you can make it more likely that the behavior will continue by using positive feedback. Positive feedback can come in a variety of forms, from a kind word to a sweet treat to a logo cap, depending on what an employee values. Whatever the reward, you should be specific and concrete about why it is being given, so the employee knows what to do again. By comparison, vague praise such as "good job!" can be misinterpreted and confusing. Behavioral psychology principles tell us that random schedules of positive reinforcement are the most powerful, so try to catch and reward an exceptional behavior when it's not expected, or when it's routine, such as a certificate handed out during the annual employee appreciation luncheon.

Similarly, whenever you notice an employee performing inappropriately, you should immediately deal with it. Don't store it and wait until formal performance review time to bring it up. The time-honored formula for correcting inappropriate behavior is DESC. You may have learned the formula during your pre-promotional management training. DESC works because it is based on the principles of behavioral psychology. Briefly, it goes like this.

DOI: 10.4324/9781003335177-10

Steps for corrective feedback:

D = Describe
E = Express
S = Specify
C = Consequences

1. Describe the Inappropriate Behavior

It's important that you focus on behaviors, or actions, rather than attitudes. For example, if you are dealing with a chronically tardy employee, you should describe the behavior concretely: "Sydney, you've shown up at least ten minutes late for your shift four times in the past two weeks." This sentence sticks to the facts.

Don't confuse observations of behavior with assumptions about what's behind them. An observation or fact is something you can check. It is either true or false. An assumption is an opinion. It is neither true nor false, it's just an opinion. If you start talking about attitudes, such as, "Sydney, you're lazy and unreliable," you are going to have trouble defending your claims. Sydney is going to deny, deflect, and defend by responding with something like, "That's just your opinion." And Sydney will be right. That conversation is doomed.

2. Express why the Behavior is Inappropriate

This step is critical because you have to come up with a good reason for requiring a change in the behavior. It's always possible that the employee didn't know that the actions are inappropriate, due to insufficient communication of expectations (see Chapter 6). Once you're sure that it's not simply a matter of clarifying your expectations, you'll need to convince the employee to change what they're doing. If you can't justify the change, your employee is unlikely to put in the effort. Sometimes managers will fall back on reasons like, "It's the policy," which sounds weak. Such statements may remind you of all the times your parents tried to correct your behavior when you were a child, justifying their demands with, "Because I said so!" You didn't think that was a good reason then, and your employee probably won't accept it now.

The following true story demonstrates the importance of expressing why a behavior is inappropriate. Once a client organization asked me to coach a manager on his communication skills. In preparation, I talked with some of his staff. Among their complaints was that every morning he set an alarm clock to go off loudly in the office at 8:00 a.m. When I asked the manager why he did that, he said it was his way of reminding the staff of the importance of promptness. They thought it was demeaning. So I asked the manager why promptness was so important, other than that it was the rule. After thinking about it for a while, he came up with a good explanation that had to do with being ready to answer the phones when the customers started calling and placing orders. Once the manager expressed this valid reason that tardiness was inappropriate, the staff's behaviors improved.

3. Specify the Behavior You Want the Employee to Adopt

Again, the emphasis here is on behaviors rather than attitudes. You must tell your employees exactly what you want them to do. That should include how often, beginning when, and with what degree of accuracy.

An example of a specific behavior to be adopted goes like this: "Beginning Monday morning, every time someone calls, please pick up the phone before the third ring and say, 'Baxter and Thompson Law Offices. Meena speaking. How may I help you?'" You can see that this statement is better than something vague like, "Answer the phone quickly and professionally."

4. Tell the Consequences of Adopting and Not Adopting the Behavior

This step may seem obvious. Most organizations have formal disciplinary procedures and policies. In one company the procedures go something like, "the first warning is oral, the second is written, the third is punished by an hour's pay deduction, the fourth is a week's suspension, and the fifth is dismissal." Employees should be well aware of the penalties for offenses. Policy and procedure manuals are supposed to include clear consequences for employee violations.

You may wonder why workers sometimes persist in doing what they know they shouldn't, such as coming in late or using office equipment for personal reasons. Behavioral psychologists have shown that human behavior can be shaped by a pattern of rewards. But what could possibly be a worker's reward for ignoring a policy and coming to work late? Well, less time spent working, for one thing – that's a major reward for some people! And if there are no negative consequences that counteract the reward, such as docked pay, the worker will be motivated to do it again. Other possible rewards for inappropriate behaviors include getting attention from the boss and/or coworkers, retribution for perceived slights, and an enhanced self-image for defying authority. Simply put, if you want a behavior to stop, figure out the reward and withhold it.

But what about the other part of step 4 – telling the consequences for correcting a behavior? "Oh, that's easy," you may say. "If the employees adopt the behaviors I expect, they get to keep their jobs." True, but is that enough motivation to make them change? Often it isn't. What usually happens is that employees try the new behavior in a goodwill effort, but as soon as they hit a bump in the road, they revert to their former behavior, despite knowing that it's inappropriate, because of the reward. It's easier to backslide than to keep trying to make the change and not getting recognized for their efforts.

> Reward subordinates when they do something right.
> Don't reward them when they do something wrong.

Are there any other rewards you can offer for compliance besides job security? You might think the only reward available is a raise in pay. But you shouldn't have to give people a raise just for doing their work correctly, which is the minimum standard for employment. Creative, skilled, respected managers know that workers are motivated by more than money; they have deep-seated needs for attention, recognition, affiliation, and approval. Therefore, saying "Thank you for this contribution to the project," and, "I liked how your presentation's opening remark brought a laugh," and, "I know how tough it was to satisfy that customer," will often be enough reward and reinforcement for maintenance of the new behavior. And if you're not sure whether pleasing you is considered rewarding, ask them what they do value. Their answer might be surprising but easy to do.

As you read in Chapter 4, positive interpersonal relationships between managers and their direct reports are powerful motivators. Can you say "thanks" too often? Probably not. The words don't lose their power to make people feel valued. Christine Porath, an expert on workplace civility, suggests that both positive and negative performance feedback should be "clear and kind," prefaced with the message, "I care about you. I know you can do better," to reduce defensiveness and signal respect.[i] Simply put, whether you want a behavior to start or continue or stop, figure out a meaningful motivation and provide it.

Formal Performance Reviews

Periodically, you are called on to conduct formal performance reviews of your direct reports. Almost 60 years ago, Maier cited several purposes for the performance review[ii] and current objectives remain much the same.

Objectives of performance reviews:

- Let employees know where they stand.
- Recognize good work.
- Communicate to subordinates how they should improve.
- Develop employees in their present jobs.
- Develop and train employees for higher jobs.
- Assess the department or unit as a whole and where each person fits into the larger picture.

While the benefits of formal performance reviews seem obvious, in fact many managers conduct them ineffectively and reluctantly. Samuel Culbert, a professor of management at the University of California-Los Angeles and author of *Get Rid of the Performance Review!*, calls it "the most ridiculous practice in the world [because] it's ... fraudulent, dishonest at its core, and reflects ... cowardly management." Culbert sees performance reviews as a way to intimidate employees and concludes that they do more harm than good.[iii]

This contradiction exists for several reasons, including that managers do not like to be put into the role of evaluator. You may fear that the discomfort created by a poorly conducted performance review will destroy your working relationship with your team. Another reason may be that managers haven't been adequately trained to conduct these interviews.[iv] If you hesitate to provide performance feedback because you fear you might drive your valuable employee to the competition, the following information will help your performance reviews have better outcomes.

Preparation considerations for performance reviews:

1   Purpose
2   Timing
3   Location
4   Content
5   Outcome

Purpose

Typically, performance reviews (1) focus on the worker's past performance, or (2) focus on the worker's future performance, including goal setting that leads to improvement. The ideal review will cover both purposes, plus two more: (3) focus on the manager's past performance, and (4) focus on the manager's future performance, including goal setting that leads to being a better boss. Thus, a formal opportunity for two-way feedback about the past and the future will benefit both parties.

As Jim Weber, CEO of Brooks Running, a part of the Berkshire Hathaway conglomerate, points out, "The whole command and control thing is a relic. It's about engaging people and creating a North Star, a purpose, so that the team is going to give as much as they get."[v]

Remember, though, that there should be no surprises in a performance review. If you've dealt with negative behaviors on the spot and rewarded positive behaviors as you caught them, and if your relationship with your employee is open and honest, then both of you will already know what will happen during a formal evaluation session.

Timing

Formal reviews are most often conducted at least once a year, with the understanding that the manager's informal feedback should be given whenever needed. There should be no surprises during a formal review because it should be a summary of all the prior conversations about positive feedback, corrective feedback, career path, and compensation.

Why perform a formal review once a year when you already provide regular, frequent feedback? Periodic "course correction" makes sense for even very satisfactory employees. Also, certain situations, such as the completion of a major project or unusually poor performance, require feedback in a formal setting. Consider the entire situation when determining the best time for a performance interview.

Once you've selected the time, tell the employees well in advance so they can prepare psychologically. Avoid the "stop by my office as soon as you get a chance" type of announcement.

Location

Once the purpose and timing are set, consider the best place for the interview. Managers tend to schedule the performance review in their own offices without realizing how potentially threatening this environment may be, especially when the worker is not accustomed to spending much time in the manager's office. Often, the best place for the interview is a neutral, safe, private location that maximizes two-way interaction.

Message Content

Next, focus on the content of the session. Regardless of the specific purpose, review the dimensions of their job, review notes from the previous performance review and recent job occurrences. You may even want to ask customers, peers, or other managers for their feedback about the employee. After gathering all your feedback documents, list specific items you want to cover in the performance review interview.

During the interview, the more you let the interviewee talk, the more likely that open and valuable communication will result. Studies show that managers who encourage a self-review of performance are more satisfying than those based strictly on manager-prepared appraisals.[vi] For useful feedback in both directions and reasonable goal setting, you must establish trust through two-way communication.

If you have lots of negative feedback to convey, you might be tempted to use the old "sandwich" format; however, it doesn't usually work. In the sandwich approach, you place a negative statement between two positive ones. Most employees quickly recognize this as manipulative and they discount the positive statements while mentally preparing a defense against the negative one. A better procedure is to begin the performance review with positive feedback and ask the employee open questions such as, "What accomplishments are you most proud of this year?" This tactic helps to establish a supportive climate and two-way interaction. Once aware that you do appreciate past success, the interviewee becomes more receptive to corrective feedback.[vii] A good transition to this part of the review is another open question such as, "What do you wish you had done differently this year?" or "What will you do when this situation happens again?" or "What tools do you need to improve your work performance?"

Outcome

At the end of the performance review, be sure that you and the interviewee compose action plans for improvement. Both of you should contribute to each other's action plans and both of you should agree on them. They should be behavior-based, specific, concrete, achievable, and challenging. To show seriousness of intent, you might each sign them. These action plans may be in addition to the employee appraisal forms that your People Operations Department expects you to complete. The key is to create a perception of a common goal that you both will work toward.

Action plan contents:

- What I will do
- When I will do it
- With whom I will do it
- What I expect to be the result
- How I will know I am successful

Performance Feedback for Culturally Diverse Workers

Formal performance review interviews are unique to US work environments. In most other countries, especially collectivist and high power difference cultures, the assumption is that workers will always give their best (Chapter 2). This attitude may be grounded in the fact that a single family often controls an entire industry. When you work for family, you continually give your best effort to make the business profitable and the family prosperous. Deep involvement and commitment make feedback from managers unnecessary.

A more complex situation occurs when workers in a US business come from one of these other cultures. For example, in a manufacturing company based in Houston, the laborers were predominantly Vietnamese, while the production managers were Anglo-American and Hispanic. The managers had difficulty getting their workers to take direction; they typically ignored both positive and negative feedback. Close observation revealed that the workers listened only to their Vietnamese elders on the shop floor. From then on, the managers simply explained to the elders what they wanted from the workers, and the elders made sure it happened.

A key concept to this approach is that "equity" is not the same as "equality." Both terms refer to the way people are treated. But "equality" means everyone is given the same resources or opportunities. "Equity" recognizes that each person has different circumstances and allocates the exact resources and opportunities needed to reach an equal outcome. Managers of culturally diverse workers should strive for equity when giving feedback.

An outstanding model of how this concept works is Jay Wright, head coach of men's basketball at Villanova University from 2001 to 2022. Widely regarded as one of the best college athletics coaches of all time, during his 21 seasons at VU he led the team to 16 NCAA Tournament appearances, six Conference championships, four Final Four appearances, and two national championships. One of the things that made Coach Wright so successful was the respectful, equitable culture he created. Put simply, he believed that "everyone's role is different but everyone's status is the same."[viii] You can foster similar workplace cultures by consistently expecting everyone's best efforts while taking care of people on every level.

Defensive and Supportive Communication Climates

In order to establish a trusting environment during the performance review and even during informal feedback sessions, you need to create and

Table 7.1 Supportive and Defensive Climates

Defensive Climate	Supportive Climate
Evaluative	Descriptive
Control	Problem orientation
Neutrality	Empathy
Superiority	Equality
Certainty	Provisionalism

maintain a supportive communication climate. Table 7.1 draws on Jack Gibbs' classic work that shows you what to say and how to say it.[ix] In the following discussion, you will see concrete examples of statements for each category in Table 7.1.

Evaluative vs. Descriptive

Communication that blames someone naturally leads to a defensive climate. Avoid statements that make moral judgments or that question their values and motives. Descriptive communication provides specific feedback, not opinions (see Table 7.2).

Control vs. Problem Orientation

Problem-oriented communication defines a mutual problem and seeks a solution. Controlling communication tries to do "something" to another person such as forcing a change in a behavior or an attitude. The problem orientation conveys respect for the employee's ability to work on a problem and to find answers to the problem.

Table 7.2 Evaluative vs. Descriptive Communication

Evaluative	Descriptive
You simply have to stop making so many silly mistakes.	We're still getting more than three errors per run with the new system.
Betty, you're tactless and rude.	Betty, some people say they are offended by your jokes.
The delay was definitely your fault because you didn't follow instructions	There seems to be some confusion about the instructions.

Table 7.3 Control vs. Problem Orientation

Control	Problem Orientation
Here is what you can do to reduce errors.	What do you think we can do to reduce errors?
You definitely have a problem with that project.	We've got a problem with this project.
Stop being so negative around here.	How do you think we could develop a more positive approach?

As you can see in Table 7.3, the problem-oriented comments develop more opportunities for two-way communication by using open-ended questions. Listening is also a productive by-product of the problem orientation.

Neutrality vs. Empathy

Neutrality expresses a lack of concern for the well-being of the employee, while empathy shows that you identify with the employee's problem, share their feelings, and accept the emotional values involved.

As the examples in Table 7.4 indicate, you show empathy during a performance review when you ask how the employee feels about something and when you attempt to understand and accept the employee's feelings.

Superiority vs. Equality

The less the psychological distance between you and the employee, the greater the probability of an effective performance review. Managers often

Table 7.4 Neutral vs. Empathic Communication

Neutrality	Empathy
That really isn't much of a problem.	Sounds like you're really concerned about it. Tell me more about the situation.
Everybody has to face that at one time or another.	That can be a tough situation. I'll tell you how I've seen it handled before, and then you can give me your reaction.
Well, everyone is entitled to an opinion.	I think we disagree. Let's discuss this further and compare viewpoints.

Table 7.5 Superiority vs. Equality

Superiority	Equality
After working on this kind of problem for 10 years, I know how to handle it.	This solution has worked before, so it should work here too.
I'm paid more than you so it is my responsibility to make this decision.	It's my ultimate responsibility to make the decision, but I sure want your recommendations.
The type of problems I face shouldn't be of interest to people at your level.	I want to share with you the type of situations I'm involved with.

stifle interviewees by subtly indicating both verbally and nonverbally their superior position, wealth, power, intelligence, or even physical characteristics. Sitting behind a big desk, looking disinterested, and acting busy, are all signs of superiority. Showing superiority can only add to defensiveness and reduce two-way communication.

Instead of telling the employee what to do, ask permission, as exemplified in Table 7.5. Instead of saying, "Rewrite this report and correct all the mistakes," try, "May I make a suggestion? I can show you an easy way to find mistakes and correct them." This approach removes the barrier of "Don't tell me what to do!"

A subtle way to communicate equality is using hedge markers. Beginning your statements with phrases such as "I think," "I feel like," "Apparently," and "It seems that" indicates that what follows is your opinion or perception. Such markers also convey an invitation to the receiver to present their own perceptions and opinions. When you begin your thoughts with a hedge marker, you're indicating confidence but not rigidity, and you're leaving an opening to them to disagree, which is gracious.[x]

Certainty vs. Provisionalism

Managers who emphasize certainty often phrase what they say as if the decision can't be changed. This dogmatic approach makes the employee feel that offering new ideas or a different solution is a waste of time. Provisionalism demonstrates that you are willing to be challenged to arrive at the best possible solution. Provisionalism promotes enthusiasm and provides a challenge to employees (see Table 7.6).

These five elements of an effective communication strategy – description, problem orientation, empathy, equality, and provisionalism – are major factors in reducing defensiveness and developing trust. Once trust has developed, your feedback is more often accepted and taken seriously.

Table 7.6 Certainty vs. Provisionalism

Certainty	Provisionalism
I know what the problem is, so there isn't much reason to talk about it.	I have some ideas, but it would be good to talk about it.
This is the way it's going to be done.	Let's try it this way for a while and see what happens.
I want it to be completed by June 1.	What needs to be done to ensure that it's completed by June 1?

Summary

"Getting it done" calls for knowing strategies for positive and corrective feedback, so you can motivate your employees to higher levels of performance. They will see feedback as constructive rather than as negative criticism if you keep in mind the following principles:

1   Describe the inappropriate behavior. Avoid criticism and claims about motives, intents, and feelings.
2   Explain why it's inappropriate.
3   Focus feedback on a limited number of observable behaviors that you want the employee to adopt.
4   Tell them what will happen if they adopt the new behavior and what will happen if they don't.

To ensure that the objectives or action plans are clear, write them down. Action plans guide employees' future activities to achieve established goals.

As a manager, you are responsible for the performance appraisal process. The challenge is to balance the needs of the organization and the needs of your staff. If you approach performance reviews fairly and without bias, you can achieve your objectives and grow your own managerial skills in the process.

Your employees are more likely to accept corrective feedback when you have created a supportive communication climate. By using a communication strategy that is descriptive, problem-oriented, empathic, equal, and provisional, you will reduce defensiveness and develop trust.

Notes

i   Christine Porath (2016). *Mastering Civility: A Manifesto for the Workplace* (New York: Grand Central Publishing), p. 92.
ii R. F. Maier (1958). *The Appraisal Interview: Objectives and Skills* (New York: John Wiley & Sons), p. 3.

iii Samuel A. Culbert (2010). *Get Rid of the Performance Review! How Companies Can Stop Intimidating, Start Managing, and Focus on What Really Matters* (Hachette Book Group).

iv B. Dugan, "Effects of Assessor Training on Information Use," Journal of Applied Psychology 73 (1988), pp. 743–48; and Timothy M. Downs, "Predictions of Communication Satisfaction During Performance Appraisal Interviews," *Management Communication Quarterly* Vol. 3, no. 13 (1990), pp. 334–54.

v David Gelles (2022, April 3). "No Longer Running but Still in the Race," *The New York Times*, p. 4.

vi B. E. Becker and R. J. Klimoski (1989). "A Field Study of the Relationship Between the Organizational Feedback Environment and Performance," *Personnel Psychology*, Vol. 42, no. 3, pp. 343–58.

vii Douglas Cederblom, "The Performance Appraisal Interview: A Review, Implications, and Suggestions," in Kevin L. Hutchinson (ed.), Readings in Organizational Communication (Dubuque, IA: Wm. C. Brown, 1992), pp. 310–21.

viii Matt Mullin (2022, April 22). "Kyle Neptune Ready to Embrace 'Monumental Task'." *The Philadelphia Inquirer*. Retrieved from https://www.inquirer.com/college-sports/villanova/live/villanova-jay-wright-retirement-kyle-neptune-fordham-20220422.html

ix Jack R. Gibb (1961, September). "Defensive Communication," *Journal of Communication*, pp. 141–48. https://doi.org/10.1111/j.1460-2466.1961.tb00344.x

x John McWhorter (2022, May 15). "'I Feel Like' There's no Problem Here." *The New York Times*, p. SR9.

Chapter 8

Strategies for Managing Conflict

"Getting it done" is all about daily workplace interactions. So far in Part 3 of this book, we've talked about how to communicate your job expectations to your direct reports (Chapter 6) and how to give them performance feedback (Chapter 7). Continuing our examination of tough communication challenges that you face every day, this chapter looks at conflict. Included are strategies for managing clashes between you and your boss, you and your teammates, and you and your direct reports.

Let's first distinguish between destructive and constructive conflict – you may be surprised to learn that conflict can benefit you and your company. Then we'll peek behind the curtain to learn why conflict is always such a strong presence, especially in diverse workplaces. Finally, and probably most important to you, we'll describe five strategies for dealing with conflict and explain when each one works best.

You're probably most familiar with destructive conflict at work, the kind that leads to communication breakdowns, negative emotions, and strained relationships, especially when the conflict is expressed in offensive comments or actions. Tensions can run high at work. As a manager, you are likely to spend up to 35 percent of your time dealing with complaints and handling disruptions in your fast-paced, diverse work environment.[i] Conflict may range from a simple disagreement over a work procedure, to an argument over priorities, to a work stoppage, and even to violence. The incidence of workplace violence continues to increase at an alarming rate. Violence is the number one cause of death on the job for women, and the number two cause for men. It's a manager's duty to protect workers from violence by developing intervention efforts.

When is conflict beneficial and when is it harmful? What causes conflict, anyway? What methods can you use to resolve conflict? Is any single method best? The following discussion answers these questions.

Pros and Cons of Workplace Conflict

Conflict generally is considered a negative influence that is destructive and is to be suppressed. Often, personal conflict comes from a worker judging

DOI: 10.4324/9781003335177-11

another's character, intelligence, personality, or worthiness. When expressed, these judgments lead to tension, arguing, and criticism, which makes everyone feel uncomfortable and undermines the work group's cohesion and productivity. Personal conflict can also affect an employee's commitment and involvement as others grow uncomfortable and feel psychologically unsafe interacting with the team.[ii]

On the other hand, conflict can be a positive influence if you manage it properly. Here are some benefits. Conflict forces you to analyze goals, creates dialogue among employees, and fosters creative solutions. It has been linked to organizational learning, and even to improved performance and productivity. Without conflict, employees and organizations would stagnate.

Conflict between diverse age groups is one example of how conflict can be positive. As discussed previously, for the first time in US history, four generations are working together. Conflict commonly is due to differences in their work style and philosophy. Older workers often view "work" as a place – a location you go to at a specified time, such as 9 a.m. to 5 p.m. Younger workers tend to view "work" as something you do – anywhere, any time. They grew up in a digital world where information is always available. So it's easy for Boomers to conclude that Millennials who arrive at 9:30 are working less hard than those who arrived at 8:30, not realizing that the younger generation may have already put in time at their home computers or smartphones while still in pajamas. To Millennials, rigid scheduling of work is unnecessary. Boomers can benefit from their younger coworkers by learning that much of today's work can be done in flextime for maximum efficiency.

Conflict also can foster creativity. Conflict helps to overcome biases by forcing you out of your traditional ways of thinking. In this way, conflict promotes the unstructured thinking that lets you develop good, novel alternatives to difficult problems.[iii] In addition, decisions are better when there is open opposition and resistance. In one study, high-quality decisions occurred in 46 percent of the situations with strong worker resistance, but in only 19 percent of the situations where resistance was weak or nonexistent.[iv]

Thus, if you are a manager who prides yourself on running a smooth ship, you may not be as effective as you think. The smooth ship may reflect suppressed conflict that could have potential benefits if allowed free play. In fact, the conflict might not be as harmful as suppressing it is.

So what's the optimal level of conflict for a collaborative work group? Whether the conflict originates from the task, the relationships, or the process, teams generally benefit from a moderate level of conflict. Too little can result in groupthink; too much can lead to team dysfunction. A moderate level of conflict allows team members to share and resolve their differences. It creates an environment where people feel heard and their ideas are valued.[v]

Benefits of workplace conflict:

- Forces goal analysis
- Creates dialogue among employees
- Fosters creative solutions
- Stimulates organizational learning
- Improves performance and productivity
- Prevents stagnation

Causes of Workplace Conflict

When you perceive conflict in the workplace, you may assume it's due to incompatible personalities. "Why can't everyone just get along?" you plead. Indeed, conflicts between workers may be grounded in personal biases, stereotypes, different work styles, or different communication styles. But if you think about it, you may find the sources of conflict are often deeper than individual personalities. Once you identify the causes, then you will be better able to select the right communication strategy for handling it.

The underlying causes of conflict often are the organization's hierarchy, ways of doing business, and a built-in opposition between units. Research shows that conflict increases with levels of hierarchy, standardization of jobs, and the number of workers.

The distribution of the limited resources available in an organization is another source of conflict. If resources were unlimited, few conflicts would arise, but this condition seldom exists. When resources are limited, and more than one person or group wants a share, conflict and competition develop.

Diverse goals are yet another source of organizational conflict. For instance, clashes may occur between quality assurance and production in a manufacturing company. The goal of the quality people is zero defects, while the goal of production is filling the customers' orders on time. Conflicting goals and roles can also explain why a company's sales people routinely ignore the accounting staff's requests for expense receipts. Or why a shift supervisor refuses to let their workers attend a training session offered by the Director of Talent Development. To reduce such traditional conflicts between functional units, managers should remind their people of the overarching goals, mission, and vision.

Sources of workplace conflict:

- The organization's hierarchy
- Ways of doing business
- Built-in opposition between units
- Highly standardized jobs
- Large number of workers
- Distribution of limited resources
- Diverse goals

Strategies for Managing Workplace Conflict

Once you have pinpointed the sources of workplace conflict, you are ready to manage the conflict. This section presents five strategies for managing conflict up the ladder of power and authority, across the ladder with peers, and down the ladder with subordinates. While reviewing these strategies, keep in mind that different conflict situations call for different strategies, so effective managerial communication means that you match the strategy to the situation.

Most of us have a favorite way of handling workplace conflict – you'll probably recognize yours when you read about it in this section, and maybe even nod in agreement. If you're not that self-aware, however, you can turn to the Conflict Resolution Survey in the Appendix of this book. Take the 30-item survey and then calculate your score for each strategy. This is your conflict resolution profile. The strategy with the highest score is your preferred approach to conflict. The second highest is the one you tend to use under pressure.

Strategies for managing conflict:

1 Avoid
2 Accommodate
3 Compromise
4 Force
5 Collaborate

Managing Conflict with Bosses: Avoid

You might think that the best way to handle conflict with your boss is to avoid it. The avoidance or withdrawal strategy combines a low concern for production with a low concern for people. If you use this style a lot, you see conflict as useless. Rather than undergo the tension and frustration of conflict, you use avoidance simply to remove yourself from conflict situations, either physically or psychologically. You dislike tension, don't take sides in a disagreement among others, and feel little commitment to any decisions reached. This conflict management style is the second most popular among US managers.

Avoidance doesn't need to be dramatic. You can avoid by ignoring a hurtful comment or quickly changing the subject when the conversation begins to threaten. Another way to avoid is to place the responsibility for an issue back on your boss. A third way to withdraw is to use a simple response of "I'm looking into the matter," with the hopes that the boss will forget the issue.

This strategy is frequently used in large bureaucratic organizations that have too many policies. Rather than tackling the conflict, you simply blame it on "policy." If you lack self-confidence in your communication abilities, you may hope the problem just disappears. However, following the dictum, "never complain, never explain," usually doesn't work in the long run. In fact, withdrawal has been negatively associated with knowledge of the boss's feelings and attitudes; open, upward communication; perceived helpfulness of the employee; and strength of the planning relationship. Thus, avoiding conflict with the boss doesn't usually make things better in critical managerial areas.[vi]

Managing Conflict with Bosses and Peers: Accommodate

The second type of conflict resolution is accommodating. You try to deal with conflict by giving in, hoping to make everyone happy. When using this approach, you emphasize maintaining relationships with bosses and coworkers, and you de-emphasize achieving productive goals. Since you are aiming for others' acceptance, you often give in to others' desires in areas that conflict with your own. You use this style if you believe confrontation is destructive.

Typical attempts to accommodate may include such things as calling for a coffee break at a tense moment, breaking the tension by cracking a joke, saying "you're right" when they're not, or engaging in some ritual show of togetherness such as an office birthday party. Since these efforts are likely to reduce feelings of conflict, they are better than simple avoidance. But handling conflict by giving in will probably have short-range effects. Just because someone does not experience a hostile or negative feeling does not mean the real cause of the conflict is resolved. In fact, accommodating is a camouflage approach that can break down at any time and create barriers to progress. Research has found that managers in low- or medium-performing organizations accommodate to reduce conflict more often than managers in high-performing organizations do.

In addition, accommodating hurts open communication with the boss and with participation in goal setting. Think of your latest performance review. Did you give in to the boss's judgments of your work quality without discussion or pushback? If so, did the boss think you had accepted the judgments as fair and true? How did you feel afterward – motivated to work harder? Probably not.

Managing Conflict with Bosses and Peers: Compromise

Compromise, the third strategy for conflict resolution up and across the organization's hierarchical ladder, assumes that half a loaf is better than none. Since compromise provides some gain for both sides rather than a unilateral victory or loss, you might judge this approach to be better than the other strategies just described.

Compromise is used when one of two conditions exists: (1) neither person thinks they can force their way on the other person, or (2) one or both people believes winning may not be worth the cost in money, time, or energy. Compromise is often highly related to negotiating, which is a legitimate conflict resolution strategy between today's workers and bosses. Compromising may make both parties think they won, but they may also both feel like losers. A negative overtone may develop in the working relationship between you and the others, and any sense of trust may break down. While everyone may have begun with a cooperative attitude, a sense of competition may be the final outcome.

A second concern with compromise is that the person with the most information has the better position, usually the person who has a better network. This power of information may restrict open communication, often resulting in a lopsided compromise. A third factor is the principle of the least-interested party: The party that has the least interest in the outcome is the more powerful person. As a result, a coworker who has little concern about your welfare or the team's welfare may have the most influence in a compromise.

Managing Conflict with Direct Reports: Force

The previous sections described traditional ways to approach conflict upward, that is, between you and your boss, and horizontally, between you and your peers at the same level of power. But what about conflict down the ladder, when you are experiencing conflict with your direct reports?

You use force when you need to meet production goals at all costs, without concern for the needs or acceptance of your employees or team. Losing is destructive because you think it reduces status, seems weak, and fosters a poor image. You must win no matter what, because winning gives you a sense of excitement and achievement.

The forcing strategy will probably cause later conflicts, however. To see the negative effect this style may have, just think about the language managers use to describe conflict: beat the opposition, battle, fight, conquer, coerce, smash, nuke. Such language and imagery can result in long-lasting, emotional wounds.

While force may resolve immediate disputes, the long-term effects will probably include a loss of productivity. Forcing in conflict situations is negatively associated with adequacy of planning, helpfulness of the supervision, and participation in goal setting. The major result of forcing is that your employees are reluctant to carry out orders because they think that the ultimate resolution of the conflict will put them on the losing side of a win–lose position.

Although forcing has limited use, research shows that managers consider forcing to be their favorite backup strategy for dealing with conflict. Immediate compliance is misperceived as a long-term solution in these cases.

Managing Conflict with Anyone: Collaborate

So far, it may seem that no totally acceptable, productive strategy exists to manage conflict. Fortunately, this is not the case. Collaborating, the fifth strategy to consider, is a win–win strategy for conflict. This complex and highly effective approach requires skillful, strategic managerial communication, but it reaps a big dividend; thus, the remainder of this section centers on the collaboration approach. Let's first describe this win–win strategy and then examine specific ways to use it.

The key is that it follows a mutual problem-solving approach rather than a combative one. In contrast to managers who use accommodating, avoiding, compromising, or forcing, managers who collaborate assume that a high quality, mutually acceptable solution is possible. Everyone directs energies toward defeating the problem and not each other.

Yes, collaborating is a complex approach that takes time and skill. Here are the five steps in the collaboration process:

1   *Define the problem.* The problem definition must be specific. Stating the problem in a conflict situation is usually much more difficult than you expect, and most people jump to solutions before they clearly define the problem. Because of this, our inclination is to state the problem as a solution rather than as a goal, which results in ambiguous communication. The outcome may be increased conflict. One helpful strategy is to write out the problem statement clearly, so everyone can see it and agree on it. Or you can agree on a problem stated as a question. State goals in the form of group goals rather than your own goals.

2   *Analyze the problem.* Again, most people want to skip this step. After all, they may argue, they live with the problem. What is the point of spending more time wallowing in it? The answer is that by exploring the depths of the problem, by looking at its history, causes, effects, and

extent, you can later come up with a solution that addresses more than symptoms, one that is more than a bandage. It will address the root cause of the problem, thus improving its chances of being successful.

3 *Brainstorm alternatives.* Everyone involved in the conflict should offer potential solutions. One idea may stimulate other ideas. The more you communicate in an open, safe environment, the greater the potential for finding effective solutions. Trust, of course, evaporates when an idea is criticized during a brainstorming session. As soon as someone says, "That's a terrible idea. It'll never work," who would be willing to take the risk of coming up with another idea? Make sure that you don't judge ideas prematurely.

4 *Develop criteria for a good solution.* These criteria, also called standards, may already be in place and available. Other times, your boss will tell you what a good solution must look like. Occasionally, you and/or your team are allowed to develop your own criteria. In work settings, the most common criteria for a good solution are as follows:

- It must be cheap
- It must be easy to do
- It must call for using resources already on hand
- It must be legal
- It must be in line with the organization's mission or values

5 *Evaluate the brainstormed alternatives using the criteria.* This is really the easiest step. By this time, you have reached agreement on the problem, and everyone has had a say about possible solutions. The best solution will appear automatically because it is the brainstormed alternative that matches your list of criteria.

Steps in the collaboration process:

1 Define the problem
2 Analyze the problem
3 Brainstorm solutions
4 Develop criteria for a good solution
5 Find the best match

You might ask, if collaborating is the best all-around strategy for resolving conflict, why don't we do it more often? The simple answer is that this process calls for two prerequisites: time and ability. You can't count on reaching a consensus on a solution right away. Hearing everyone out takes time and patience, commodities that are rare in today's workplace.

Secondly, the participants have to know how to collaborate; they must be familiar with, and be willing to follow, the five steps just described.

Here's a true story that illustrates the importance of these two pre-requisites for conflict resolution. Once I had a graduate student who managed the third shift in a manufacturing company. After attending my evening class from 6:00 to 9:00 p.m., Rob would head off to work from 11:00 p.m. to 7:00 a.m. Before class one evening, Rob told me that two of his crew had been locked in conflict for some time over a tools issue, and so he had tried using the collaborative strategy that he had learned in my class. "How did it go?" I asked eagerly. Rob reported, "It didn't work." He had put his employees into the break room and said, "Come out when you two have reached an agreement." After an hour, they had returned to the line, saying they'd worked it out, but Rob said they hadn't used collaboration. When I asked what approach they had used, he told me, "Seniority." The worker who had been on the job longer got their way.

This example demonstrates the importance of training people on the steps in the collaboration strategy for conflict resolution. It's based on how we think when we are trying to rationally solve a problem, but participants must know and stick to the steps in the process for it to work.

The preceding paragraphs presented five strategies for managing conflict in the workplace. After reviewing these strategies, keep in mind that different conflict situations call for different strategies, so effective managerial communication means that you know how to match the strategy to the situation. Table 8.1 will help you find the best approach.

Develop a Positive Communication Climate

Heterogeneous work teams almost inevitably experience conflict. Power levels may be pretty equitable among team members, and relationships may be weak due to cultural differences and/or geographic distances. Here are some strategies for teams to turn potentially destructive conflict into constructive conflict.

Set Ground Rules Around How Team Members Express Disagreement

As a team, discuss and decide on rules for how to have a productive disagreement and discourage personal conflict. Be sure everyone is familiar with the rules. Some common team rules are as follows:

- Be specific and give reasons why you disagree.
- Offer revisions or friendly amendments to other's ideas.
- Communicate respectfully – name-calling, insults, or personal criticisms are out of bounds.

Table 8.1 When to Use Each Conflict Resolution Strategy

Conflict Resolution Strategy	When it Works Best	Result
Avoiding	• There's little chance you'll get your way • The potential damage of addressing the conflict outweighs the benefits of resolution • People need a chance to cool down • Others are in a better position to resolve the conflict • The problem will go away by itself	I lose You lose
Accommodating	• Preserving harmony is important • Personal antagonism is the major source of conflict • The issue itself is unsolvable • You care more about the relationship than getting your way	I lose You win
Compromising	• Two opponents are equal in power • Temporary settlements on complex issues are needed • Opponents do not share goals • Forcing or problem solving won't work	I half win, half lose You half win, half lose
Forcing	• Quick, decisive action is needed, as in a crisis • A rule has to be enforced • You know you're right • You must protect yourself	I win You lose
Collaborating	• Both sets of concerns are too important to be compromised • It is important to work through hard feelings • Commitment to the resolution is important • A permanent solution is desired	I win You win

- Give the benefit of the doubt; don't assume other people's motives for disagreeing with your idea.
- Recognize that disagreement can be used as an opportunity to clarify or improve an idea.

Embrace Differences in Style, Background, and Perspective Among Team Members

Acknowledge that team members think, communicate, and solve problems differently from one another, and show how you value those differences.

Make it clear that having members with different perspectives and ways of expressing themselves is a benefit to the team's mission. You can also help to bridge or find connections between different viewpoints.

Invest Time in Relationship-building

Conflict is often caused by a lack of understanding about why someone thinks or acts the way they do. Take time to build positive relationships among team members. For instance, at the beginning of a meeting, you could ask each team member to share something about themselves that is relevant to the team or that explains how they like to work with others. This exercise will help create a team culture of mutual respect and open communication.

Encourage Team Members to Hold One Another Accountable for Following the Team's Ground Rules

Encourage team members to speak up when they see behaviors or communication straying from the team's rules, especially during disagreements. Emphasize that speaking up does not involve accusing or shaming someone.[vii]

In short, the elements that are essential for managers to navigate team conflict are regular and in-depth exchanges of ideas, the ability to maintain a respectful atmosphere, and ongoing investments in building personal relationships and trust.[viii]

Negotiation as a Conflict Resolution Strategy

Let's say that you have reflected on the source of conflict and determined that it is more than a personality clash or a disagreement of ideas. Furthermore, let's say you've addressed the situation by applying one of the five conflict resolution strategies outlined earlier in this chapter, but the conflict remains. If the conflict is between valued, high-performing team members, it may be time to try negotiation.

A simple tool called "When you, then I" can be used when negotiating conflict. The tool helps each person own their part of the conflict and expresses what they want to happen. There are three steps:

a   Describe the behavior without judgment. State what you saw or heard the other person do. Avoid using any language that judges the behavior or makes assumptions about the person.

Example: "When you interrupted me in the meeting, I was not able to finish sharing my thoughts."

b Describe the way the behavior affected you. Be factual and avoid making judgments.

> Example: "When someone interrupts me, I feel like my opinion is less important than theirs. Also, I get embarrassed."

c Make a request. State directly, but politely, what you want the other person to do.

> Example: "I would appreciate it if you would let me finish my thought before you speak."

Now it's the other person's turn to speak. Encourage them to use the "When you, then I" format to explain their behavior. Once everyone's behaviors and the consequences have been aired, seek common ground, such as the team's project goals. As a final step, negotiate an action plan that everyone can agree to as they go forward.[ix]

Summary

To help you "get it done," this chapter focuses on strategies for managing conflict. Conflict is inevitable in the workplace, and it's even more powerful a factor when the workforce is diverse. You will be able to successfully deal with conflict by following the steps described here: read the situation to identify the source of the conflict, recognize when the conflict is constructive or destructive, select the right strategy out of your toolbox, and then apply it. Negotiation may also be an effective strategy, especially when high-performing team members are experiencing conflict. To limit destructive conflict, managers should work toward creating and maintaining a positive communication climate.

Notes

i Larry A. Erbert (2014). "Antagonistic and Non-Antagonistic Dialectical Contradictions in Organizational Conflict," *International Journal of Business Communication*, Vol. 51, no. 2, pp. 138–158.

ii B.A. Stipleman, E. Rice, A.L. Vogel, and K.L. Hall (2019). "Comprehensive Collaboration Plans: Practical Considerations Spanning Across Individual Collaborators to Institutional Supports," in Kara L. Hall, Amanda L. Vogel, & Robert T. Croyle (eds.), *Strategies for Team Science Success* (Springer), pp. 587(2014) 611. DOI: 10.1007/978-3-030-20992-6_45.

iii Linda Putnam and S. Wilson (1988). "Argumentation and Bargaining Strategies as Discriminators of Integrative and Distributive Outcomes," in A. Rahim (ed.), *Managing Conflict: An Interdisciplinary Approach* (New York: Praeger Publishers).

iv L. R. Hoffman, E. Harburg, and N. R. F. Meier (1962). "Differences and Disagreements as Factors in Creative Problem-Solving," *Journal of Abnormal and Social Psychology*, Vol. 64, no. 2, pp. 206–224.

v Gail Fann Thomas (2020, November). "Perspective: Managing Virtual Team Conflict," *The Western ABC Bulletin*, Vol. 2, no. 2. Association for Business Communication. Retrieved from https://abcwest.org.

vi W. A. Donohue, M. E. Diez, and R. B. Stahl (1983). "New Directions in Negotiations Research," in R. N. Bostrom (ed.), *Communication Yearbook 7* (Beverly Hills, CA: Sage Publications), pp. 249–279.

vii "Negotiating Personal Conflict Tip Sheet" (2021). Patient-Centered Outcomes Research Institute. Retrieved from www.pcori.org.

viii L. M. Bennett and H. Gadlin (2012). "Collaboration and Team Science: From Theory to Practice," *Journal of Investigative Medicine*, Vol. 60, no. 5, pp. 768–775. DOI: 10.231/JIM.0b013e318250871d2019.

ix Jennifer R. Veltsos and G. E. Hynes (2022). *Managerial Communication: Strategies and Applications*, 8th ed. (Thousand Oaks, CA: SAGE Publications), pp. 366–385.

Chapter 9

Strategies for Detecting Deception

As we've said, "getting it done" is all about daily workplace interactions that you as a manager need to navigate. So far in this part of the book, we've talked about how to give clear directives (Chapter 6) and how to give performance feedback (Chapter 7). Continuing our examination of a manager's daily communication challenges, Chapter 8 looked at conflict and offered five strategies for managing it. This chapter focuses on another major communication challenge – analyzing nonverbal behaviors to figure out whether someone is withholding information or lying to you.

The Importance of Nonverbal Cues

How often do you find yourself wondering whether the data your employees work with are accurate? While the data set out in a report can usually be tested objectively, information you get from face-to-face interactions such as disciplinary and pre-employment screening interviews aren't always checked for accuracy. Fortunately, some nonverbal cues can help you decide whether what people are saying to you is true.

As you read in Chapter 4, nonverbal cues usually reinforce or repeat verbal ones and are used to reduce the uncertainty in communication. On the other hand, nonverbal cues might contradict the verbal ones they accompany. When you are listening to someone and what they say contradicts how they look, which do you believe? For instance, if a speaker says, "I'm delighted to be here," while she mops her brow, wads up her notes, and gulps water, do you really think she's "delighted"?

Similarly, when a manager says that the customer always comes first, but then reprimands employees for taking too much time with a customer, the actions are what employees believe – not the words. As you read in Chapter 5, inconsistency between verbal and nonverbal messages appears deceptive and generates distrust, while consistency between words and behavior builds trust.

DOI: 10.4324/9781003335177-12

When what you say contradicts how you look, people believe how you look.

Contradictory nonverbal cues that indicate deception are called leakage. When someone is lying, certain types of nonverbal cues often escape despite the speaker's attempts to control them. The subconscious apparently betrays the speaker through this nonverbal leakage. Listeners and observers read and interpret these signals, often subconsciously. That, in a nutshell, is how you can learn to spot nonverbal signs of deception.

Several patterns of nonverbal behavior crop up when someone is lying. Since you can control some sources of nonverbal cues better than others—for example, blushing is a physiological effect of lying and therefore subconscious—we will focus on cues that most people don't think about when sending messages. These include movement and gestures, manipulation of clothing, personal space, environmental artifacts, and voice.

Misinterpretation of Nonverbal Cues

Before exploring ways to tell from the nonverbal signals whether someone is lying, a word of caution is in order. You may remember from Chapter 4 that nonverbal behavior usually suggests meaning rather than having a one-to-one connection with a specific word or idea. A nonverbal cue might actually mean something different than you think it means for important reasons, such as cultural differences, and a gesture might be motivated by something other than what you assumed.

Here's an example of how easily gestures can be misinterpreted. Let's say you're wrapping up a meeting with the team at your company's Honduras site, and you decide to signal that you are happy about the outcome, so you connect your thumb and forefinger in a circle and hold the other fingers straight, indicating the word *okay*. Others in the room react emotionally, thinking you are not happy with the meeting at all, because people in much of Latin America may consider this gesture to be obscene.

In addition to gestures, norms for personal space differ significantly across cultures, too. In the United States, people typically are most comfortable engaging in social conversations when they are 3 to 5 feet apart, about arm's reach. A recent study found that Japanese and German college students preferred larger interpersonal distances, with the Japanese more comfortable even farther apart than the German students. This effect cannot be explained by body height, as the German sample was taller, and greater height is associated with larger interpersonal distances. Gender appeared to influence personal space, too; pairs of females, as compared to males, were associated with smaller interpersonal distances across ethnic groups.[i]

Continuing our overview of norms for nonverbal behavior that vary across cultures, let's briefly consider physical contact in the workplace. In contemporary US business environments, when greeting someone, acceptable touching is often limited to a brief handshake. By comparison, in some other cultures, greetings among business professionals will normally include hugging and kissing. For Muslim and Arab women, shaking hands, hugging, and kissing outside the family are taboo; they greet others by putting their right hands to their hearts with a slight bow. During business interactions, touching someone is expected in the Albanian-speaking world. Albanians get quite close when they converse, and for them it is normal to touch one another while they are talking. Very often this is done to attract the other's attention and promote collegiality.[ii]

Eye contact offers another category of nonverbal behavior that varies across cultures and is easily misinterpreted. The mainstream US business culture equates direct eye contact with honesty. We think that speakers who don't look at us while speaking have "shifty eyes" and are hiding something. We trust people who will "look us in the eye." Many other cultures, however, think that direct eye contact is vulgar and disrespectful.[iii] Within the United States, eye contact patterns differ among African-Americans, Native Americans, and Anglo-Americans. Patterns differ between men and women in the United States, too – women generally look less while speaking and more while listening than men do. Power and status often affect eye contact patterns, since gaze indicates dominance in the US business world.

In Asian countries, workers typically gaze downward when interacting with their bosses, indicating respect for authority. Japanese audiences may actually close their eyes when they are listening intently to a speech. In the United States, if an audience's eyes are closed, the speaker has likely put them to sleep.

To summarize, when analyzing the meanings of nonverbal cues, we should take into consideration the following factors: (a) Context: body language depends on the context. For example, depending on the context, you might rub your eyes to indicate irritation, being tired, upset, or disagreeing with the speaker. (b) Evidence: A single nonverbal cue is not as reliable as several cues. Clusters of signals provide a much more reliable indication of meaning than one or two signals in isolation. (c) Culture: norms, rules, language, and customs dramatically influence the meanings of nonverbal cues.[iv]

To analyze nonverbal cues, consider the following:

- Context
- Evidence
- Culture

Having said that nonverbal cues are always important in daily communication, that nonverbal cues are easily misinterpreted, and that some nonverbal behaviors can be controlled better than others, we are now ready to discuss strategies for detecting deception.

Position

To detect possible nonverbal signs of deception, it is important to be in the right place. Often, employees sit behind desks or stand behind equipment, so significant cues are hidden. The face, always likely to be visible, can be a poor source of deception cues (although hand-to-face contacts are valuable cues). When possible, position the other person in an open chair facing you, or standing where you can see them full on. Nonverbal signs from the hands, trunk, legs, or feet will then be more evident.[v] For virtual interactions using video-teleconference software such as Zoom, Skype, Slack, Adobe Connect, Google Hangouts, or Teams, you might suggest that participants use ear buds or a headset and sit back a bit from their computer so you can see more than their faces.

Baseline Nonverbal Cues

Once positioned for maximum observation of nonverbal cues, you are ready to determine baseline behavior. The theory is that deception cues are behaviors that are different from normal nonverbal cues. Therefore, you need to know what behavior is normal for that individual – their *baseline*. Researchers have found that when observers see someone giving honest answers before giving dishonest answers, the observers' ability to detect the dishonesty increases significantly compared to when there was no behavioral baseline. According to psychologist Paul Ekman of the University of California–San Francisco, you don't detect dishonesty by looking for the lie, but by noticing a change in behavior that suggests a person is nervous when they shouldn't be.[vi]

The individual's baseline is also invaluable because one person might behave differently from others in the same circumstances. A baseline allows you to tell if nervous behavior reflects the overall situation or if it's a reaction to the question you asked. Of course, deviation from their baseline might also relate to the difficulty of the question. It is possible that some may react differently when asked a question that is "right in their wheelhouse" versus one that is unexpected or challenging. Also, more personal questions might elicit a different cue simply because the respondent is uncomfortable with the topic. In general, however, nonverbal behaviors that differ from the norm can be considered indicators of deception.

Table 9.1 Nonverbal Signs of Deception

Unexpected movements and gestures
Manipulation of clothing
Increase of personal space
Misleading artifacts
Vocal variations

In a job interview, a baseline is relatively easy. At the opening, you should greet the applicant and make small talk, asking nonthreatening questions about the weather, their trip, a big sports event, and the like. Once you've settled into the interview, begin asking questions about the résumé rather than jumping right into tougher questions. Watch for baseline nonverbal cues.

If you are investigating a safety violation or similar event on the job, your interrogation could use the same pattern. Small talk serves its traditional primary purpose of putting the other person at ease and a secondary one of providing a baseline of nonverbal behavior.

The next sections explore some typical nonverbal signs of deception found in the US business environment or variations from the baseline nonverbal behaviors. They are summarized in Table 9.1.

Movements and Gestures

Gestures and trunk movements are probably the most valuable nonverbal signs of deception. Perhaps the most common deception-related gestures are the hand-to-face movements, and the most common of these is the mouth cover. More subtle is the single finger to the mouth, the moustache stroke, or the nose rub. Other gestures suggesting deception are nail biting and lip biting. Hiding the hands by putting them in pockets or pulling shirtsleeves down to the fingertips are a sign that the person is "hiding" something more than their hands.

Conversational gestures also vary from the baseline when an individual is being deceptive. Generally, when someone is comfortable and giving honest responses, their gestures are open and outward. During deception, most people both limit their gestures and keep them closer to the body. Smiling decreases and the frequency of gestures used to illustrate conversational points slows down, but the gestures suggesting deception increase. One of these is the hand shrug. Researchers have found that when individuals are lying they will shrug their hands – turning the palms up from palms down position – twice as frequently as when they are telling the truth. This cue suggests a subconscious pleading for the listener to believe what they are saying.[vii]

Some authorities also observed that an increase in leg and foot movements may indicate deception. Foot tapping, leg rocking while the legs are crossed, and frequent shifts in leg posture are examples of this kind of activity. A rhythmic "walking" motion with one crossed leg is a classic movement that suggests the person would like to walk away.

In addition to hand and leg movements, researchers have noted that a speaker's head movements can indicate deception. An example comes from the famous General Motors case concerning their cars' faulty ignition switches. In 2014, GM announced the recall of 3.2 million vehicles and paid \$35 million in penalties after an 11-year history of accidents, injuries, and deaths related to defective ignition switches. The manufacturer routinely stated that their top priority was safety, but external investigators found that the corporate culture actually valued cost control the most. In one report, there is a discussion of the "GM nod." As Mary Barra, CEO, described it, the GM nod is when everyone nods in agreement to a proposed plan of action, but then leaves the room with no intention to follow through, making the nod a deceptive sign.[viii]

Table 9.2 summarizes the movements of different body segments that you should look for when trying to detect deception. But always keep in mind the need to compare behavior with the baseline.

After reviewing deception movements, we turn to other categories. Yes, signs of deception are not confined to the body. They can involve dress, personal space, artifacts, and voice, as discussed in the next paragraphs.

Table 9.2 Deceptive Movements

Body Segment	Movement	Interpretation
Head	Shifting, darting eyes	Uncertain; lying
	Eyebrows up	Challenging
	Head down	Defensive
Trunk, shoulders	Leaning away	Skeptical
	Slouched	Low self-esteem
	Shrunken chest	Threatened
Hands, arms	Touching self, stroking hair	Nervous; anxious
	Repetitive movements	Lying; unsure of self
	Hand over mouth while speaking	Wants to escape
	Arms crossed	Protective; closed
	Hands on hips	Challenging, combative
	Hands in pockets	Secretive
	Palms hidden	Distrustful
	Pointing	Aggressive
	Clenched hands; picking cuticle	Needs reassurance

Manipulation of Clothing

Regarding dress, nonverbal leakage mainly shows up in the way individuals handle their clothes, which may suggest that they feel threatened by a certain question or topic. Someone may suddenly close and button their jacket or begin to tug nervously at a pants leg, skirt hem, or collar. Some people may pull their sleeves down over their hands or tuck their clothes tighter around their laps, betraying a fear of having some deception uncovered. Other signals include straightening or tugging at clothing, smoothing a tie, picking at lint, or rubbing at a spot.

Clothing and accessories are sometimes selected in an attempt to convey status, membership in a group, or credibility. For instance, in workplaces where uniforms are standard, individuals may select expensive footwear or jewelry to scale up from the standard appearance, thereby projecting a superior position in the hierarchy. Politicians campaigning for election, on the other hand, may scale down their clothing to project "sameness" with a blue-collar audience. But whenever one's clothing choices are false they are likely to be uncomfortable, which leads to manipulation of the outfit, ultimately signaling a lack of authenticity.[ix]

Personal Space

The distance that someone keeps from others as well as their relation to the surrounding environment may be a rich source of deception cues, though it is culture specific. An employee or job applicant might shift the chair's position or might suddenly lean back on the chair's rear legs. In the United States, these forms of moving away from you may show a lack of co-operativeness, or it might be a feeble attempt to put distance between themselves and you by changing the environment. In the United States, when a person in a conversation physically backs up, the other person typically comes closer. In stand-up conversations, if an individual is giving a deceptive response to your question, they may lean back or step back and try to prevent you from bridging the gap by "blocking" with a piece of furniture, an object, or even by folding their arms across their chest.

An employee or applicant who has been relaxed may tense under pressure. In the United States, if a tense person suddenly crosses their arms and legs and leans back, you can interpret this change as deceptive. A forward posture is less comfortable when fearing discovery, and the individual may be feeling vulnerable and defensive. The person may also try to erect *signal blunders* to hide behind. These may be such subtle activities as placing a file, notebook, or briefcase in the lap as a barrier. On the other hand, if you notice that an individual "opens up" physically during a response and leans toward you, you might interpret the nonverbal cue as an indication of trust, openness, and honesty.

Misleading Artifacts

Personal possessions in the workplace and the physical environment itself offer cues, and they can be manipulated to create the intended impression. Some people will meticulously decorate their offices or cubicles in an attempt to manage the perceptions of their visitors. Although many of these decorations can reflect honest identity claims, some can be strategic and even deceptive.[x] How many times has a car salesperson lured you back to their office after viewing some vehicles in the showroom, where you notice a variety of framed family photos is on display? Such artifacts seem to say, "You can trust me. I'm family-oriented. I would never give you a bad deal." Excessively showcasing awards, plaques, framed certificates, and photos taken with celebrities on a "brag wall" is another common attempt at self-promotion. Personal effects in the office can serve as clues to who the real person is, but you should question their authenticity.

The following true story illustrates the importance of artifacts as nonverbal cues in the workplace. Once I was hired to coach the owner of a freight company on her interpersonal communication skills. She told me that she had inherited the business from her late husband, and she was having difficulty getting the employees to take her seriously. Everyone ignored her directives, she complained. She wanted to be recognized and respected as a leader.

As she talked, I glanced around her office. I saw piles of clothing and shoes, foam plastic clamshells of leftover take-out meals, half-empty coffee cups, stacks of files and papers in disarray. The chairs and tables were covered with clutter. When her phone rang, she had difficulty finding it on the desk. No wonder people didn't listen to her. She didn't seem to be able to manage her office, let alone her business. I helped her realize that if she wanted her employees to respect her as a competent leader, her environment had to reflect her competence. As a side benefit, gaining control over her physical surroundings by organizing her artifacts gave her new confidence in her abilities.

Voice

Voice is another rich source of cues. Everyone's voice is unique. That's how you can tell who is calling when you hear them say "hello" on the phone. Just as we learned in our review of movement and gestures, any unexpected changes from baseline vocal behaviors can indicate deception. Furthermore, there are patterns of vocal style that we come to expect from people, and when those patterns vary from the norm, we should become suspicious.

When what you say contradicts how you sound, people believe how you sound.

Think of the people in your workgroup. Because you meet regularly, you've come to expect that Elise speaks first, speaks fast, and speaks loudly about every agenda item. When someone tries to interrupt, she keeps talking, faster and louder. On this particular agenda item, however, which is relevant to her team's current project, she has remained strangely silent. When you ask for the relevant data, she hesitates before responding and then rambles about how hard her team is working. You follow up by asking whether there will be a problem meeting the project's deadline. Slowly, again, and with an increasingly strident pitch, she says, "Of course not. My people have always come through, haven't they? Don't you remember the Croft account fiasco that we narrowly avoided just because my team pulled together over that long weekend?" Should you be worried? Possibly. On the other hand, if Elise has a good track record, her response might reflect that she hasn't worked out precisely how she will meet the deadline. Her denial might just mean, "Please trust me to take care of this. Don't micromanage. I've got it." When interpreting nonverbal signals, knowing the context clearly helps.

A recent study examined CEO speech samples that were taken as they interacted with financial analysts and investors during earnings conference calls or video disclosures of corporate forecasts. The researchers compared the CEOs' vocal styles when talking about positive and negative corporate news and found significant differences between the executives' baseline vocal styles and deceptive vocal styles. The study indicates that the most relevant vocal cues for deception are pitch, tone, and volume, as well as the response's start and length. Deceptive answers typically have a slower start than honest ones. In addition, deceptive answers are likely to be longer and less specific than honest ones. The deceiver may be attempting to fill in the gap with needless material. Length may be seen as an attempt to make a deceptive statement more elaborate and thus more convincing than the deceiver knows it is. A statement's length may also reflect the pauses, throat clearings, and hesitations needed as the speaker stumbles through the answer.[xi]

Pitch is another important source of deception. Researchers have found that a speaker's pitch rises measurably in deceptive responses. While observers frequently could not say why they labeled such a response as deceptive, they knew it was, and research instruments revealed the pitch difference.[xii]

Vocal aspects of deception:

- Pitch
- Tone
- Volume
- Onset
- Duration

In summary, if you suspect that someone is hiding information or deceiving you, consider their nonverbal communication behavior in these categories: movement, gestures, clothing, personal space, artifacts, and vocal style. Look for variations from their baseline behaviors. Your conclusions are likely to be more accurate if you "have an experienced eye for the unexpected."[xiii]

Summary

Strategies for "getting it done" include tuning in to the nonverbal messages that coworkers, staff, bosses, job candidates, and other stakeholders communicate. When managers interact with employees and potential employees, nonverbal cues are the source of most of the message. While not everything communicated nonverbally is done so consciously or intentionally, the unintentional signals may be as valid as the intentional ones and are potentially more useful in deciding whether the person is being honest or deceptive.

Keep in mind, though, the suggestions about establishing a behavioral baseline for each person in specific situations. Then simply watch and listen for sudden deviations. In addition, if you suspect deception, use that as a sign that you need to investigate further, and as a sign of caution. Don't jump to conclusions or take your perceptions as the final word. Remember to factor in cultural differences and the possibility that a particular conversation topic has caused the speaker to become self-conscious, tense, or emotional.

Notes

i Maurizio Sicorello, Jasmina Stevanov, Hiroshi Ashida, and Heiko Hecht (2019). "Effect of Gaze on Personal Space: A Japanese–German Cross-Cultural Study," *Journal of Cross-Cultural Psychology,* Vol. 50, no. 1, pp. 8–21. DOI: 10.1177/0022 022118798513.

ii Brikena Kadazdaj and Vjosa Hamiti (2020). "Nonverbal Communication in German-Albanian Cultural Contrast," *Sakarya University Journal of Education,* 10, no. 1, pp. 187–201. DOI:10.19126/suje.689503.

iii Sicorello (2019).

iv Ibrahim A. Abu-Arquoub and F.A. Alserhan (2019). "Non-Verbal Barriers to Effective Intercultural Communication," *Utopía Y Praxis Latinoamericana,* Vol. 24, no. 5, pp. 307–316.

v John L. Waltman (1983, June). "Nonverbal Interrogation: Some Applications," *Journal of Police Science and Administration,* Vol. 11, no. 2, p. 167.

vi Jeff Gammage (2006, January 29). "Good Liars May be Wired Differently," *Houston Chronicle,* p. 2D.

vii Charles J. McClintock and Raymond G. Hunt (1975). "Nonverbal Indicators of Affect and Deception in Interview Situations," *Journal of Applied Psychology,* Vol. 5, no. 3, p. 420.

viii Anton R. Valukas (2014). "Report to Board of Directors of General Motors Company Regarding Ignition Switch Recalls," p. 250.

ix Dana R. Carney (2021, February). "Ten Things Every Manager Should Know about Nonverbal Behavior," *California Management Review,* Vol. 63, no. 2, pp. 5–22.

x Sam Gosling (2008). *Snoop: What Your Stuff Says About You* (Profile Books), p. 13.

xi Alfredo Contreras, Aiyesha Dey, and Claire Hill (2020). "'Tone at the Top' and the Communication of Corporate Values: Lost in Translation?" *Seattle University Law Review*, Vol. 43, no. 2, pp. 497–523.

xii Mark L. Knapp and Mathew S. McGlone (2016). *Lying + Deception in Human Interaction*, 2nd ed. (Dubuque, IA: Kendall Hunt).

xiii Abu-Arquoub and Alserhan, p. 312.

Part IV

Get Ahead

Chapter 10

Trends in the Global Workplace

Let's review for a moment. This book is designed to help you "get along, get it done, and get ahead" at work. Chapter 3 in Part I introduced you to the Sequence for Success model that is at the heart of the book (Figure 10.1). The model illustrates how interpersonal communication behavior leads to strong work relationships, which build loyalty, satisfaction, and commitment. These positive emotions, in turn, lead to maximum performance and organizational success.

In Part II, you read about strategies for "getting along." You learned best practices for communicating up, down, and across the hierarchy. You were introduced to communication behaviors that will help you find out what's going on and what people are thinking. You also learned how to build a strong organizational culture, characterized by trusting relationships that allow you to understand and influence coworkers' actions.

Part III presented strategies for "getting it done." You discovered best practices for communicating job expectations to your workers and giving performance feedback. You learned strategies for managing conflict with the boss as well as conflict among your work group. And you learned ways to tell when someone is withholding information or lying to you.

Now here we are at Part IV, ready to look into your professional future. "Getting ahead" requires tuning in to major trends in the global work environment and aligning with their implications. This chapter identifies four of these trends and offers ways to get onboard. Then you will know how to thrive in tomorrow's workplace, which is the subject of Chapter 11.

Trends

As you manage your career path, you will want to consider four major trends in the global work environment: increased reliance on technology, more reliance on teams and collaboration, expanded workforce diversity, and heightened emphasis on ethics. Table 10.1 summarizes the trends and introduces implications for your success as a manager.

DOI: 10.4324/9781003335177-14

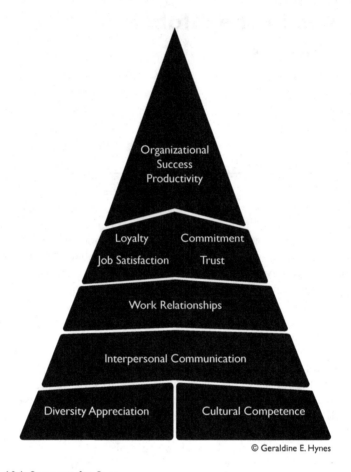

© Geraldine E. Hynes

Figure 10.1 Sequence for Success.

Table 10.1 Trends in Global Business and Implications for Managers

Trend	What to Do About It?
Increased reliance on technology	• Become media sensitive
	• Guide employees' use of technology
Increased reliance on teams and collaboration	• Use social media/collaboration tools
	• Provide training
Increased workforce diversity	• Learn another language
	• Create a welcoming culture
Increased emphasis on ethics	• Develop a formal code of conduct
	• Broadcast it to everyone

1. Increased Reliance on Technology

If you spend as much time as most managers do reading and responding to email, texting your staff, blogging both internally and with external stakeholders, participating in podcasts, webinars and virtual meetings, and compulsively checking your mobile device while sitting in traffic, you know that developments in technology will drive the future of business. In the words of Tom Friedman, columnist for the *New York Times* and winner of three Pulitzer Prizes, we have gone from a connected world to a hyperconnected world in the last ten years.

Advantages of technology:

- Increased efficiency
- Increased productivity
- Improved communication

Remote Work

The COVID-19 pandemic that began in 2020 accelerated an experiment in a different way of working – some 50 million Americans left their offices and went home. In 2019, about 4 percent of employed people in the United States worked exclusively from home; by May 2020, that figure rose to 43 percent overall, and to 65 percent for white-collar workers.

As COVID cases declined in 2022 and restrictions eased, many corporations began requiring their employees to return to the workplace. Goldman Sachs, JPMorgan Chase, American Express, Meta, Microsoft, Ford Motor, and Citigroup are just a handful of the companies that started bringing workers back. Not surprisingly, they've been met with resistance. According to Youngjoo Cha, a sociologist at Indiana University, "We had a nationwide experiment in telecommuting. These conditions challenged the notion of ideal workers."[i]

A recent survey from management consultancy Advanced Workplace Associates showed that only 3 percent of white-collar employees prefer to work in the office five days a week, and 86 percent want to work from home at least two days a week.[ii] Studies of 10,000 office workers conducted by Future Forum in 2021 suggest that women and people of color were more likely to see working remotely as beneficial than their white male colleagues. In the United States, 86 percent of Hispanic and 81 percent of Black knowledge workers said that they preferred hybrid or remote work, compared with 75 percent of white knowledge workers. And globally, 50 percent of working mothers who participated in the studies reported wanting to work remotely most or all the time.[iii]

How strongly do workers feel about working remotely? Blind, an app allowing anonymous career-related posts, surveyed 3000 employees at Apple, Amazon, Google, Facebook, Microsoft, Goldman Sachs, and JP Morgan. An astonishing 64 percent of the survey respondents said they are willing to sacrifice US$30,000 in raises to keep the option of working remotely.[iv]

Clearly, organizations that try to satisfy the demand for remote work options are dependent on reliable technology. On the other hand, those workers who are back in the workplace also depend on communication technology; for one thing, that means Zoom meetings will remain a central aspect of the day. It can be easier than corralling a group into a conference room, and in some cases, it's a necessity for teams working across different cities or countries. There are additional benefits of video calls, compared to in-person meetings. It's easier to look at documents or notes on a screen alongside the call. The screen-sharing function means there's no need to print out pages. And Zoom meetings with clients and stakeholders in other locations save travel time and money.

The primary justifications for the increased reliance on pandemic-era technology are improved efficiency, productivity, employee morale, and timely communication. But technology is more than a beneficial tool; it's a force that managers must constantly reassess. Technology is not always good just because it's new. It requires some creative thinking to strike a balance between technological advantages and workplace relationships.

Disadvantages of technology:

- Sensory overload
- Weak work relationships
- Reduced feedback

Media Sensitivity

The previous paragraphs point to a future where networked organizations remain the norm. Therefore, the strategic decision for you is not whether to use technological channels but which channel is best for a situation and how you can maximize its capabilities.

As a manager, you shouldn't simply rely on the channel you feel most comfortable with when communicating; you need to consider the impression the channel makes with your intended audience. Here is a true story that demonstrates this idea. Once there was an accounting department manager who relied exclusively on sticky notes for communicating with her direct reports, to the extent that she would silently enter a worker's cubicle, stick the note onto the computer monitor, and silently leave again, while the employee sat right there. Why do you think she routinely used this communication tool? How do you think the employees felt about the manager and her messages?

You must decide when to use technology and when to speak in person with your intended audience. Different situations and messages call for different channels, as illustrated in Table 10.2.

Why should you care about channel choice? Because it's a key to achieving your communication goal as well as your professional success. Several studies have identified a strong correlation between a manager's media sensitivity and managerial performance. For instance, when a task

Table 10.2 Channel Options for Messages

Message Type	Message Example	Key Channel Characteristics	Channel Example
Sensitive	Condolence	Broad bandwidth Feedback mechanism Symbolic importance	In-person
Negative	Layoff	Broad bandwidth Feedback mechanism	In-person Videoconference
Complex	Procedure	Permanence Feedback mechanism	Multiple channels
Routine	Meeting reminder	Low cost Efficiency	Email blast Text message
Persuasive	Sales	Broad bandwidth Interactive Symbolic importance Feedback mechanism	In-person Videoconference
Need for immediate response	Question	Feedback mechanism Speed	Text message Instant message In-person Phone call
Informative	New product	Permanence Accessibility Broad bandwidth	Blog Email attachment Newsletter

involved complex information or was highly emotional, effective managers were more inclined than ineffective managers to use communication channels with a broad bandwidth, or capacity to carry information, such as in-person conversation.[v] So if you want to be successful at work, you should work toward becoming media sensitive.

> Successful managers are media-sensitive managers.

Media sensitivity includes guiding your employees in the proper, ethical use of communication technology. For instance, Instant Messaging is an official corporate communication tool for over one-fourth of US companies. Employees use IM on their own in another 44 percent of companies, sometimes for personal as well as business-related communication. Yet 35 percent of companies don't have an official IM policy, risking breaches of confidentiality, viruses, and copyright infringement.[vi] New communication tools are constantly becoming available, requiring strategic decisions about their use. Your people rely on you for training and for modeling ethical use of technology.

Media Surveillance

A second, related prediction about communication technology is that monitoring mechanisms will become increasingly sophisticated. Surveillance methods are developing right along with innovations in technology. For example, federal law enforcement and national security offices have sweeping authority to monitor Internet communications, including encrypted emails, social networking websites, and peer-to-peer software such as Skype and Zoom. In the United States, phone and broadband networks are already required to have interception capabilities under a 1994 law called the Communications Assistance to Law Enforcement Act. These capabilities apply to companies that operate from servers abroad and that conduct international business.

The business sector has surveillance privileges that are similar to the government's, allowing them to eavesdrop on employees. Electronic monitoring systems allow employers to gather very detailed information about how their employees spend their time at work.[vii] Companies monitor employees for many reasons. These include the following:

- Preventing lawsuits
- Reducing the misuse of company resources
- Protecting intellectual property[viii]

Companies have invested in technology that can do much more than block access to certain Internet sites. Companies may routinely backup and archive emails, install keylogging software to record keystrokes and time spent at the keyboard, use router logs to monitor Internet traffic, even put global positioning systems on employees' badges to record workers' movements.[ix]

> **Assume your technology use at work is being monitored.**

Furthermore, employers don't have to alert employees to the fact that they are watching. Secret monitoring is widespread and supported by the courts. Surveillance has resulted in employees being reprimanded or fired for improperly using company-provided Internet, emailing inappropriate or offensive messages, and violating confidentiality rules.[x] Perhaps surprisingly, a majority of people in the United States consider surveillance to prevent theft and monitor performance to be acceptable.[xi]

Your employees should realize that any time spent using technology at work should be limited to work-related activities. Further, any messages they send or receive at work should be appropriate for anyone to read. In 2010, in its first ruling on the privacy rights of employees who send messages on the job, the Supreme Court unanimously agreed that supervisors may read through employees' text messages if they suspect that work rules are being violated. So warn your people to be on their best behavior and to think twice before doing something questionable while on the job.

2. Increased Reliance on Teams and Collaboration

Job trends research confirms that collaboration and teamwork are among the top ten critical work skills for the future.[xii] In fact, 90 percent of all US businesses and 100 percent of Fortune 500 companies use some form of group structure already. Their need for collaboration lies in the complexity and interdependence of tasks, which make it difficult for one person to have enough information to make decisions and solve problems in today's organizations.

It's easy to see why teams have been adopted as a key work structure in contemporary organizations. Today's workplace is fast-paced and intense. The traditional management hierarchy is often clumsy and slow in responding to changes in the marketplace. So many organizations have replaced a bureaucratic hierarchy with flexible, cooperative, mission-driven teams led by managers who expect their direct reports to participate fully in the task or project at hand. If you are this kind of manager, you encourage collaboration and group loyalty among your team members every day. The focus is on using two-way communication to encourage input and keep everyone informed, thereby creating a sense of community and a collaborative culture.

> Virtual teams use social media tools to support collaboration.

Communication challenges are greater when your employees are on the road, geographically scattered, working from home, or on flexible schedules. Marc Cenedella, the founder of Ladders, a career site for positions paying US$100,000 or more, recommends that remote teams gather in-person at least once a quarter or so, to meet one another and provide a chance for workers to connect with colleagues.[xiii]

If in-person interactions are not practical, however, you can use social enterprise tools such as Facebook at Work, Yammer, or Jive to connect people. Streaming video and instant messaging are well suited to building community. A 2013 survey of 651 organizations in a range of industries and global regions found that the majority of employers (56 percent) use social media to communicate with employees on topics such as organizational culture, team building, change management, and innovation. Furthermore, 70 percent of the survey respondents agreed that the use of internal social business/collaboration tools had a positive impact on employee productivity.[xiv]

The more managers use these tools, the more adept they become at fostering collaboration. When employees connect, either in-person or through technologies, they can establish dialogues and collaboration rather than relying on top-down communication. The manager of the future must know how to support collaboration.

Leading Teams

Managing teams calls for special leadership skills. First, it's important to select team members who communicate information freely and honestly. Once your team is in place, here are some other strategies that will support collaboration:

- *Be a facilitator.* Managing teams is less about supervising than it is about motivating members to do their best. Avoid the tendency to micromanage once you have defined the team's objectives and responsibilities.
- *Support the team.* Provide resources, run interference, and resolve internal conflicts. Give them all the information they need, and more, to encourage trust. Remember that people cannot work in a vacuum.
- *Delegate.* Managers occasionally have trouble admitting that they cannot do it all. Instead of trying to manage every aspect of a meeting

or project, trust members to perform their assigned tasks. This trust also builds respect for you as a leader and maintains morale.

- *Seek diversity.* Heterogeneous groups experience more conflict but often produce higher-quality results than homogeneous groups. Stress the importance of collaboration, flexibility, and openness toward unfamiliar viewpoints and work styles.[xv]

DIVERSITY =
Different **I**ndividuals **V**aluing **E**ach other
Regardless of **S**kin, **I**ntellect, **T**alents, or **Y**ears

In teams or work groups that are culturally diverse, you may have to deal with communication difficulties and language barriers, which decrease cohesion. Be sure your people put teammates at ease by respecting the conventions of each culture. Writing styles, for example, differ across cultures. A direct, concise email may be standard in the United States, but Japanese recipients may consider it rude and vulgar. That's why an email I recently sent to a colleague at a Japanese university began with, "The local cherry blossoms are particularly beautiful this spring."

Fluency may be a roadblock for transnational team members communicating in English. As the team leader, you can build in more time during teleconferences and perhaps hire translators. Nonverbal behavior also varies from culture to culture, as you read in Chapter 4. For example, in the United States, business professionals usually shake hands when they "seal a deal," but unrelated men and women are forbidden to touch in Islamic countries. Even when using videoconferencing tools that allow your team to see each other's nonverbal cues of posture, facial expression, and voice tone, the risk of misunderstanding remains strong. As a manager, you must decide whether these more expensive methods of communication are worth the attempt to reduce the assumptions and barriers involved. DEIA (diversity, equity, inclusion, and accessibility) training programs can reduce the likelihood of misunderstandings and blunders among your team.

3. Increased Workforce Diversity

A third trend that will impact your success as a manager is the expanding diversity of the workforce. As the workforce becomes more diverse, your communication skills will become more important than ever.

Types of Diversity

The data confirm what everyone has already noticed in their own orga-nization – diversity is a reality along the dimensions of gender, age, edu-cation, and culture. Even in Silicon Valley, where high-tech firms were once known as being a bastion of white and Asian men, efforts are being made to attract more women, Latinos, and Black/African-Americans. Why? Because companies that value DEIA tend to be more creative and more profitable. Varied perspectives help them design products and services that have global appeal.

You may be especially sensitive to issues of age diversity if you su-pervise workers older than you are. The percentage of those over 65 who have remained in the workforce has been rising steadily since the 1990s. The US Census Bureau projects the portion of those 65 and older who are working will grow to 23 percent by 2022. Astoundingly, almost 20 percent of 70–74 year olds are currently still working. And it's likely that they will want you to interact with them respectfully, just because of their age and experience. Since the payoff of a diverse workforce depends not on the diversity itself but on promoting a sense of be-longing, you must use tact when managing people who may be your parents' (or grandparents') ages.

Culturally Sensitive Communication

Despite the fact that diverse workforces are the norm, a 2014 Towers Watson Global Workforce Study shows that only about half of today's managers are viewed as effective by their direct reports when it comes to their skill at listening to different points of view and working across cultural differences.[xvi] Clearly the gap must be closed. The strategies described in Parts II and III of this book will help you develop a welcoming culture that values individuals regardless of ethnicity, intellect, talents, gender, or years. As a manager, you must be able to connect with others in a deep and direct way and develop relationships that will bridge differences.

Tips for managing work teams:

- Be a facilitator
- Support the team
- Delegate
- Seek diversity

Bridging differences takes social and emotional intelligence, as you read in Chapter 4. Cross-cultural competence involves awareness of differences and the ability to capitalize on those differences.

Linguistic skills strongly affect cultural awareness. In her autobiography, US Supreme Court Justice Sonia Sotomayor describes her struggles as a child in the South Bronx – she spoke only Spanish at home but attended classes taught only in English. Sotomayor argues that language is "a code of the soul" that unlocks the music, poetry, history, and literature of a culture, "but it is also a prison." Teachers lacking knowledge of Spanish language and culture, for example, didn't realize that Hispanic kids who looked down when scolded were doing so out of respect, as they'd been taught. This nonverbal behavior only invited more scolding: "Look at me when I speak to you!"

Speech and language differences, nonverbal behavior such as eye contact, and facial expressions all complicate the communication process in cross-cultural situations. Misunderstandings and communication breakdowns may also be due to differences in the degree of directness, appropriate subjects for conversation, touch, loudness and pitch, even silence. As a Yankee living in Texas, I had firsthand experience with cultural differences regarding proximity. At first my students, both male and female, surprised me by hugging me in greeting whenever I saw them on campus. Because it makes me uncomfortable, I advised them that where I come from, students don't hug their professors. But they just laughed, pointing out that I'm not in Chicago anymore. So I devised a scheme of hugging from the side to minimize the invasion of my personal space without insulting them.

Justice Sotomayor learned early "that things break down [when] people can't imagine someone else's point of view."[xvii] Learning at least a little about another language is a practical way to improve interpersonal communication on the job. Beyond that, it's a way to continue your education and manage your career. Learning another language indicates that you are aware of and accept another culture's values, traditions, and worldview.

In summary, to improve your communication with culturally diverse workers:

- Check for possible language differences as the source of misunderstanding
- Look for possible cultural sources of misunderstanding
- Acknowledge your communication mistakes and correct them
- Correct others' inappropriate communication behavior

4. Heightened Emphasis on Ethics

If you paid any attention at all to the major corporate scandals in the early 21st century, you know how dangerous unethical behavior can be.

Executives at Adelphia, Arthur Andersen, Enron, WorldCom, Martha Stewart Omnimedia, HealthSouth, and other corporations were charged with major ethics violations – accounting fraud, stock manipulation, obstructing justice, lying, and so on. Many of the accused executives were convicted, and some of their companies were even destroyed. In June 2022, Ernst & Young, a major accounting firm, agreed to pay US$100 million in fines after hundreds of its auditors were found to have cheated on various ethics exams they were required to obtain or maintain professional licenses. This is the largest penalty the US Securities and Exchange Commission has ever imposed against a firm in the auditing profession.[xviii]

Publicized scandals have resulted in expanded concern for ethical standards in business. The Sarbanes-Oxley Act of 2002 requires companies to develop a code of ethics applicable to employees and directors. Today, 95 percent of both the Fortune US 100 and Fortune Global 100 companies publish a code of ethics or conduct or a values statement. Furthermore, a majority of the Fortune 100 companies that have a code of conduct extend it to vendors and contractor companies.[xix] In general, a code of conduct is a formal document intended to guide corporate, employee and other stakeholders' behavior. A code of conduct is different from a mission statement in that a mission statement declares what the organization intends to accomplish, while an ethical code spells out the values embraced by the organization.

Sarbanes-Oxley also makes corporate leaders responsible for the unethical behavior of their employees – unless they can show that they provided adequate ethical training for them. As a result, 79 percent of the Fortune 100 companies require employee training on their code of ethics, with proof of completion.[xx] Thus, it's important that managers adhere to their organization's ethical code daily while also making sure their direct reports do the same.

You face ethical dilemmas and temptations every day. Ethical issues range from corporate accounting practices to social media use by employees, harassment, and pay equity. We discussed the importance of trust and a positive communication climate in Chapter 5. Unfortunately, it's difficult to develop trust when so many blatant examples of mistrust occur and when you face conflicting ethical demands. The only way to build trust is to consistently follow the practices of ethical communication.

> The only way to build trust is to follow the practices of ethical communication.

If your company has not developed a formal code of ethics, check to see whether your professional association has. For instance, the American Society for Quality specifies standards for behavior of quality management professionals. The Institute for Supply Management also developed a code of ethics relevant to supply chain managers' challenges. And the Project Management Institute not only has a Code of Ethics and Professional Conduct posted on its website, it even offers its 700,000 global members a downloadable "code values card" in 18 languages.

Alternatively, you can compose a code of conduct for yourself and your work group, perhaps with input from your People Operations and Legal Departments. The code should clarify standards for employee conduct and state that you expect your people to recognize the ethical dimensions of their workplace behavior and communication. The code may be broad or specific regarding values, but at a minimum, it should address managerial communication, align with your organization's regulatory and legal contexts, and reflect sensitivity to cultural differences. It should also spell out the consequences of noncompliance with the standards. Finally, you should broadcast your code to all employees and regularly check that they understand it.

My Code of Conduct

Let me give you a personal example of a code of conduct. I am a longtime member of the Association for Business Communication, an international organization committed to fostering excellence in business communication research, education, and practice. ABC publishes its members' code of conduct and guiding principles on its website. These principles are truthfulness, honesty, and fairness; confidentiality; integrity; and professional and social responsibility. The code specifies valuing diversity, practicing inclusion, and treating others with respect.[xxi]

Here's one way that ABC's Code of Conduct applies to my own professional activities. The section on confidentiality states, "We protect our clients' proprietary, personal, and organizational information. We do not divulge information, concepts, or findings … [in] conference papers, proceedings, or journal articles."[xxii] The implication of this professional standard is that, when I come across a document that exemplifies a business writing principle, I only use that document as a "real world" example after the writer's client company has given permission. I sanitize it, too, so curious students or readers can't figure out where it came from. That's how my Code of Conduct works to ensure that my practices as an author, consultant, executive coach, and professor are ethical.

Summary

This chapter provides a look into the future. In order to "get ahead" managers should tune in to major trends in the global work environment. Four of these trends are identified and ways to get onboard are suggested: increasing reliance on technology, growing reliance on teams and collaboration, expanding workforce diversity, and heightened emphasis on ethics.

The justification for our increasing reliance on technology is increased efficiency and productivity, but technology has both advantages and disadvantages. When messages are sensitive, negative, nonroutine, and/or complex, face-to-face interactions may be preferable to technology. Surveillance of employees' use of technology will continue to grow.

A second trend, the growing emphasis on collaboration, calls for managers' ability to use social media as a way to share information, thereby building community.

A third trend, expanding gender, age, education, and cultural diversity in the workplace, requires that managers improve their sensitivity by becoming familiar with others' practices, principles, languages, and preferences. Similarly, managers should help their employees develop appreciation for DEIA through training.

A fourth trend toward heightened emphasis on ethics requires that managers create or support a code of conduct and broadcast it to everyone in the organization. Managers face ethical dilemmas and temptations every day, and the only way to maintain trust and integrity is to consistently follow an established code.

Notes

i Emma Goldberg (2022, March 10). "A Two-Year, 50-Million-Person Experiment in Changing How We Work," *The New York Times*. Retrieved from https://www.nytimes.com/2022/03/10/business/remote-work-office-life.html.

ii Claire Ballentine and A. McNeely (2022, April 1). "Employees Are Returning to the Office, Just to Sit on Zoom Calls," *Bloomberg Wealth*. Retrieved from https://www.bloomberg.com/news/articles/2022-04-01/employees-are-returning-to-office-post-covid-just-to-sit-on-zoom-calls.

iii Sheela Subramanian (2021, March 11). "A New Era of Workplace Inclusion: Moving From Retrofit to Redesign," *Future Forum* blog. Retrieved from https://futureforum.com/2021/03/11/dismantling-the-office-moving-from-retrofit-to-redesign/.

iv Jack Kelly (2021, May 21). "Survey Asks Employees at Top U.S. Companies if They'd Give Up $30,000 to WFH: The Answer May Surprise You." *Forbes*. Retrieved from https://www.forbes.com/sites/jackkelly/2021/05/21/survey-asks-employees-at-top-us-companies-if-theyd-give-up-30000-to-work-from-home-the-answers-may-surprise-you/?sh=55749769330f.

v Gail S. Russ, Richard L. Daft, and Robert H. Lengel (1990, November). "Media Selection and Managerial Characteristics in Organizational Communications," *Management Communication Quarterly*, Vol. 4, no. 2, pp. 151–175.

vi "The Present (and Future) of Business Communications," (July 25, 2005). *Accounting Web*. Retrieved from http://www.accountingweb.com.

vii H. Joseph Wen, D. Schwieger, and P. Gershuny (2007). "Internet Usage Monitoring in the Workplace: Its Legal Challenges and Implementation Strategies," *Information Systems Management*, Vol. 24, no. 2, pp. 185–196.

viii D. Elmuti and H. H. Davis (2006). "Not Worth the Bad Will," *Industrial Management, 48*(6), 26–30.

ix A. D. Moore (2000). "Employee Monitoring and Computer Technology: Evaluative Surveillance v. Privacy," *Business Ethics Quarterly*, Vol. 10, no. 3, pp. 697–709.

x American Management Association (2019, April 8). "The Latest on Workplace Monitoring and Surveillance." Retrieved from https://www.amanet.org/articles/the-latest-on-workplace-monitoring-and-surveillance.

xi Lee Rainie and M. Duggan (2016, January 14). "Privacy and Information Sharing," Pew Research Center. Retrieved from http://www.pewinternet.org/2016/01/14/privacy-and-information-sharing

xii Institute for the Future (2011). *Future Work Skills 2020*. Institute for the Future for the University of Phoenix Research Institute. Retrieved from www.iftf.org.

xiii *The Ladders Quarterly Remote Work Report* (2022). Retrieved from https://www.theladders.com/wp-content/uploads/Ladders-Inc-Q1-2022-Quarterly-Work-Report.pdf

xiv Towers Watson (2013). *Change and Communication ROI Study – The 10th Anniversary Report*. Retrieved from www.towerswatson.com

xv Liz Hughes (2004, January-February). "Do's and Don'ts of Effective Team Leadership," *WIB, Magazine of the American Business Women's Association*, p. 10.

xvi Towers Watson (2013).

xvii Sonia Sotomayor (2014). *My Beloved World* (New York: Vintage Books), pp. 199, 123.

xviii Matthew Goldstein (2022, June 28). "Ernst & Young to Pay $100 Million Fine After Auditors Cheated on Ethics Exams," *The New York Times*. Retrieved from https://www.nytimes.com/2022/06/28/business/ernst-young-sec-cheating.html

xix M. Babri, B. Davidson, and S. Helin (2021). "An Updated Inquiry into the Study of Corporate Codes of Ethics: 2005–2016." *Journal of Business Ethics*, Vol. 168, pp. 71–108. Retrieved from https://doi.org/10.1007/s10551-019-04192-x

xx Robert Rasberry (2013, March 15). "A Study of How Fortune 100 Companies Communicate Ethics, Governance, Corporate Responsibility, Sustainability, and Human Rights." Paper presented at the Association for Business Communication-Southwestern U.S. Annual Conference, Albuquerque, NM.

xxi Association for Business Communication (2005). "Professional Ethics – Code of Conduct." Retrieved from https://www.businesscommunication.org/p/cm/ld/fid=258.

xxii Association for Business Communication (2005). "Professional Ethics – Code of Conduct."

Chapter 11

Strategies for Thriving in the Global Workplace

Part IV is all about taking care of your career. Chapter 10 identified four major trends for you to keep in mind when preparing yourself for success in tomorrow's global business environment:

- Increasing reliance on technology
- Increasing reliance on teams and collaboration
- Increasing diversity in the workforce
- Increasing emphasis on ethics

This chapter narrows the focus to what is arguably the toughest but most important strategy for professional success – developing your cultural sensitivity – and offers tools to help you reach that goal. Further, it presents ideas for developing cultural sensitivity among your employees or work team, so they, too, can be successful in a diverse workplace.

Self-Assessment Tools

Before you can reach your goal, you have to identify where you are now. Self-assessment can be an uncomfortable process, but it's the way forward.

The Diversity Awareness Continuum

Here is a quick and easy tool for determining your starting point in developing cultural sensitivity (Table 11.1). Read and react to each sentence in the left-hand column by putting an X in one of the middle column spaces that best reflects where you fit. Then draw your profile by connecting your Xs.

Now that you know the starting point, it's easy to find your endpoint or goal. The closer your line is to the right-hand column, the greater your awareness regarding diversity. The closer to the left-hand column, the less aware you may be about diversity-related issues. Your goal is to move closer to the right-hand column on each dimension.

DOI: 10.4324/9781003335177-15

Table 11.1 Diversity Awareness Continuum

	1	2	3	4	5	
I don't know about the cultural norms of different groups in my organization.	___	___	___	___	___	I know about the cultural norms of different groups in my organization.
I don't hold stereotypes about other groups.	___	___	___	___	___	I admit my stereotypes about other groups.
I feel partial to, and more comfortable with, some groups than others.	___	___	___	___	___	I feel equally comfortable with all groups.
I gravitate toward others who are like me.	___	___	___	___	___	I gravitate toward others who are different from me.
I prefer managing a homogeneous team.	___	___	___	___	___	I prefer managing a multicultural team.
I feel that everyone is the same, with similar values and preferences.	___	___	___	___	___	I feel that everyone is unique, with different values and preferences.
I'm confused by the culturally different behaviors I see among staff.	___	___	___	___	___	I understand the cultural influences behind some of the behaviors I see among staff.
I get irritated when confronted by someone who does not speak English.	___	___	___	___	___	I show patience and understanding with limited English speakers.
I'm task focused and don't like to waste time chatting.	___	___	___	___	___	I find that more gets done when I spend time on relationships first.
I feel that newcomers to this society should comply with our rules.	___	___	___	___	___	I feel that both newcomers and their employer organizations need to change to fit together.

Bennett's Model

Figure 11.1 presents another tool you might find useful for self-assessment. Milton Bennett designed a six-stage developmental model of cultural sensitivity.

You will note that the first three stages are "ethnocentric": *denial, defense,* and *minimization.* An example of a *denial* statement is, "No matter where you go, a smile will open all doors." At the second stage, *defense,* you are aware of differences but hostile toward other cultures, so you might say, "Our way is the right way." At the third stage, *minimization,* the differences you are aware of are superficial, so you might say something like, "When dining with my Chinese coworker, I'll use chopsticks."

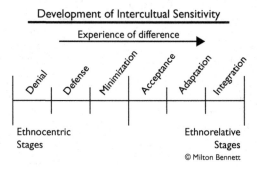

Figure 11.1 Bennett's Model.

Ethnocentric managers may acknowledge the existence of cultural differences but see their culture as the best in the world and look down on others as inferior because they are different. For whatever reasons, the ethnocentric manager builds resentment rather than good relationships.

Stages of ethnocentrism:

1 Denial
2 Defense
3 Minimization

On the other hand, Bennett identified three ethnorelative stages: *acceptance, adaptation,* and *integration* (Figure 11.1). An example of a statement by a manager at the *acceptance* stage is, "I see why we have belief differences," or "Differences are OK." If you are at Bennett's *adaptation* stage, you can empathize, so you might say something like, "I will adopt some aspects of a culture," or "Differences enhance the workplace." If you are at his *integration* stage, you have developed the ability to embrace and capitalize on differences. An example statement at this stage is, "We're not a melting pot. Let's go for the stir-fry."

Stages of ethnorelativism:

4 Acceptance
5 Adaptation
6 Integration

Ethnocentricity	"Our way is the right way."
Awareness	"There may be another way."
Understanding	"I see why there are differences."
Acceptance	"Differences are OK."
Valuing	"Differences enhance the workplace."
Adoption	"I can pick what I like from a culture."
Multiculturalism	"We're not a melting pot. Let's go for the stir-fry."

Figure 11.2 Developing Cultural Sensitivity.

An ethnorelativistic manager recognizes and respects cultural differences and finds ways to make the workplace amenable to all.[i] Try plotting your course for cultural sensitivity by identifying where you are on the flowchart (Figure 11.2), which is based on Bennett's model.

How Culturally Competent Managers Behave

Let's say that through self-assessment and experience you've developed a level of cultural sensitivity. How does that manifest in your daily workplace behavior? In other words, how can you walk the talk? Michael Morris, a business professor at Columbia University, recognizes the common pitfalls managers face when trying to treat all employees fairly and respectfully. At one extreme, a manager may take the *universalist* approach, treating all employees the same. At the other extreme, a manager may take the *particularist* approach, adjusting the treatment according to the worker's culture. Both behaviors can have a negative effect on employees' perception of justice. "If justice issues are not well-managed in a diverse workplace, detrimental consequences ranging from poor morale and turnover to intergroup rivalry and balkanization may result."[ii]

Morris offers 10 ways managers can create a welcoming culture for diverse workers:

1 Rely on multiethnic strategies, not just on good intentions. For instance, you might implement a mentoring program to ensure that all employees develop important relationships.
2 Provide every employee constructive feedback so she/he may learn and grow.

3   Work to ensure that all cultural groups have access to opportunities.
4   Work to ensure that all cultural groups perceive that they are treated fairly.
5   Provide cultural competence training to supervisors who conduct performance reviews.
6   Monitor cultural boundaries to avoid intergroup competition.
7   Manage misunderstandings by making staff aware that cultural differences may be the root cause of clashes rather than personality differences.
8   Be sensitive to obstacles facing members of certain cultural groups and be flexible about performance evaluations to even the playing field.
9   Call on those with cultural expertise.
10   Include all employees and all cultures in DEIA discussions.

A management tactic used at a Houston, Texas, manufacturing company was described in Chapter 7. It bears revisiting because it exemplifies some of Morris's suggestions for creating a welcoming culture. At the Houston facility, the workforce was predominantly Vietnamese and the shift leader was Mexican-American. The shift leader recognized that in the Vietnamese culture the elders are greatly respected and obeyed, so the leader funneled messages through the eldest workers rather than giving orders and corrective feedback directly to the younger employees. This two-step system was successful because the shift leader acknowledged and respected the cultural values of the Vietnamese workers.

According to the US Bureau of Labor Statistics, 57 percent of the workforce is female and 37 percent are people of color.[iii] These percentages are steadily increasing. Some industries, however, still fail to attract and keep women and minorities. Why? When investigating the reasons that women and minorities leave jobs in the technology industry, researchers found that the most frequently cited reason was a hostile culture. Therefore, cultural sensitivity has taken on an urgency, both in hiring and keeping multicultural workers and in reaching the multicultural consumer market. Managing diversity is every manager's challenge.

Additional Managerial Competencies

What other things will tomorrow's work environment expect from its managers? Taking a broader perspective, we find that cultural sensitivity is fundamental, but additional competencies will contribute significantly to success. Consider the following guidelines for thriving in the global economy of the future:

1   *Accept ambiguity and uncertainty.* Respect the fact that change is constant, and you will have to be flexible.

2   *Reflect and think before acting.* As you manage multicultural teams and projects, be mindful and careful before acting or reacting. Sometimes, a thoughtless disregard of cultural values can create problems.

3   *Be creative and hardworking.* Effort, commitment, and innovative thinking are prerequisites for success. Be willing to take risks and keep trying.

4   *Be a lifelong learner.* Continuing education and professional development are worthwhile investments because growth ensures success for both you and your organization.[iv]

We know for sure that tomorrow's business environment will be different from that of today. Embracing change is not an option, it's a requirement.

Your Improvement Plan

You may have nodded your head as you read the previous paragraphs. "Yes, these are all worthy goals," you may have thought. "I see the importance of cultural competence, emotional intelligence, embracing change, lifelong learning, etc. for my future success. I'm convinced. Now, how can I get there?" Simply put, you will get there by taking one step at a time. Your personal improvement plan will work if it is action-oriented and ongoing.

Here's a suggestion: At the beginning of each month, sit down and write out three things you plan to do that month – one new action for professional improvement, one for personal improvement, and one for relationship improvement. Next to each new behavior write down in what situation and with whom you will do it. Table 11.2 shows you how to organize your personal improvement plan. It also might be helpful to look at the more elaborate work plan template in Appendix 3 at the back of this book. It shouldn't take you more than about ten minutes to construct one.

On the last day of next month, check your list to see how well you met those three goals. If you didn't, try to figure out why not. Then, construct a new action plan consisting of three things you plan to do the following month, taking into account the roadblocks from last month. This system should keep you on track for developing competencies that are important for your career.

Table 11.2 My Action Plan for the Month

	Goal	Who	When	Where	What I'll Say/Do
Professional					
Personal					
Relationship					

Developing Culturally Sensitive Employees

Once you've worked on your own cultural competence, it's time to address your employees' cultural sensitivity. You don't have to send your staff overseas to develop their cultural sensitivity. The next paragraphs present several practical steps you can take to help your workforce move toward this goal.

"Well," you might say. "I can just send them to a cross-cultural communication training program." Yes, that's a good plan if a solid training program is available and the budget allows it. However, a recent study published by The Economist Intelligence Unit found that almost half of US companies don't invest in such training, though they recognize the benefits of overcoming cultural and communication barriers.[v]

Until all organizations acknowledge the need for culturally competent workers by committing more resources to formal training, managers can take some practical steps that will foster a respectful culture. Do these regularly:

- *Acknowledge the presence of culture differences.* Talk about differences in beliefs, values, goals, behaviors, and language. Try to understand and explain the reasons for these differences.
- *Insist on a respectful environment.* Be a role model by always using DEIA-sensitive language yourself. Monitor others' language, humor, and stories and point out the impact of insensitive and offensive talk.
- *Create and maintain heterogeneous teams.* Be sure to consider a range of factors when forming diverse work groups.

This last step bears some elaboration. What are some of the factors to consider when creating heterogeneous teams? After reading this far, you've probably already thought of demographic factors such as ethnicity, gender, and age. In addition, think about creating teams with differing career stages, experience in past collaborations with other team members, professional expertise, points of view, and communication style. Even a characteristic like emotional engagement in the work/project or in the team itself is important to consider. Why? Because all these dimensions of difference will have a major influence on how the team interacts when generating ideas, solving problems, and resolving conflict. These aspects of team member diversity will influence how the team functions and ultimately, the quality of the end products.

The optimal team makeup will vary by team and problem, but, in general, high-performing collaborative work teams are diverse on many characteristics.[vi] Managers and team leaders of high-performing work groups promote the benefits of DEIA daily. They encourage multiple viewpoints while discouraging groupthink and authoritarian decision making. They appreciate their team's differences, build trust, and find common ground.

When diverse teams must work in a virtual environment, they face additional challenges, especially under the stresses of a pandemic. Recent research has identified key skills for diverse team members and their leaders who collaborate virtually. Strategies for developing these skills have been suggested throughout this book. The key skills are as follows:

1 Media – knowing when and how to use specific media
2 Communication – information sharing; an ability to send and interpret messages appropriately
3 Trust – ability to develop and maintain responsiveness, dependability, active and frequent participation
4 Cultural competence – knowledge and skills to enhance interaction with people from different cultures
5 Self-management – skills to manage oneself effectively
6 Conflict management – skills to effectively manage conflict[vii]

How to encourage employees' cultural competence:

- Acknowledge cultural differences
- Insist on a respectful environment
- Create and maintain heterogeneous teams

The Bottom Line: Culturally Sensitive Managerial Communication

Developing cultural sensitivity in yourself and your people is an ongoing process. The platform that fosters this process is daily interpersonal communication. A look to the future reveals a continued strong relationship between diverse work groups, effective interpersonal communication, and organizational success. In fact, companies with highly effective communicators are three and a half times more likely to significantly outperform their industry peers than firms whose leaders are poor communicators.[viii]

What does "effective communication" mean in a culturally diverse context? It begins with a deep understanding of the organization's culture and the workers' cultures, because that knowledge allows leaders to create messages that will drive worker behaviors toward the organization's goals. A Towers Watson survey of 651 organizations worldwide found that in highly effective organizations,

- 96 percent of managers act in support of the organization's vision and values

- 93 percent of managers deliver messages in a way that is meaningful for their work group
- 91 percent of managers work across cultural differences when determining procedures
- 90 percent of managers listen carefully to different points of view[ix]

Data published by a Project Management Institute study indicate even more behaviors that distinguish effective business communicators:

- They communicate frequently with their staff about goals, budgets, schedules, and business benefits
- They communicate with sufficient clarity and detail
- They use non-technical language
- They tailor messages to different stakeholder groups
- They use appropriate settings or media[x]

Remember the Sequence for Success model that was introduced in Chapter 3 and referred to throughout this book? The model illustrates how your daily communication leads to strong relationships. These relationships lead to loyalty, satisfaction, and commitment. In turn, these emotional conditions lead to productivity and organizational success (Figure 11.3).

The model is a good place to end because it captures the central message of this book: tomorrow's managers will thrive in a global environment if they are skillful communicators, emotionally intelligent, collaborative, and culturally competent. The Sequence for Success is your guide; it will enable you to use your effective communication skills to produce the bottom-line results that make you a winner.

Summary

In order to thrive in the diverse business environment of tomorrow, managers must be culturally sensitive. Improving your cultural sensitivity begins with self-awareness. This chapter presented two tools that will facilitate self-assessment of cultural sensitivity and help you set realistic, concrete goals. Next, we considered ways to translate cultural attitudes and values into managerial behaviors. Instead of a universalist approach, which calls for treating everyone the same, or a particularist approach, which calls for individual treatment, managers need to be flexible and accommodate the cultural values and practices of the workforce.

Finally, we examined strategies for developing cultural sensitivity in others, which include formal training, zero-tolerance for disrespect, openly discussing differences, and promoting the benefits of DEIA. Following the Sequence for Success will enable you to use your effective communication skills to make you and your organization successful.

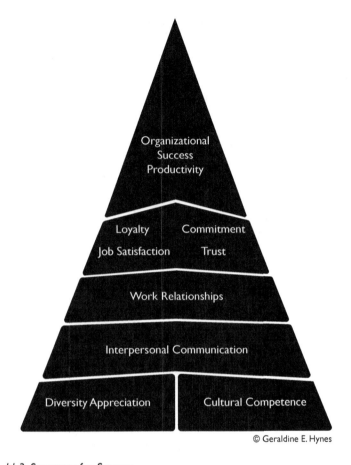

© Geraldine E. Hynes

Figure 11.3 Sequence for Success.

Notes

i Milton J. Bennett (1986). "A Developmental Approach to Training for Intercultural Sensitivity," *International Journal of Intercultural Relations,* Vol. 10, pp. 179–196.
ii Michael Morris and K. Leung (2000). "Justice for All? Progress in Research on Cultural Variation in the Psychology of Distributive and Procedural Justice," *Applied Psychology: An International Review,* Vol. 49, no. 1, pp. 100–132.
iii U.S. Bureau of Labor Statistics (2021, November). "Labor Force Characteristics by Race and Ethnicity, 2020. *BLS Reports.* Retrieved from https://www.bls.gov/opub/reports/race-and-ethnicity/2020/home.htm.
iv Wallace V. Schmidt, R. N. Conaway, S. S. Easton, and W. J. Wardrope (2007). *Communicating Globally: Intercultural Communication and International Business* (Thousand Oaks, CA: Sage Publications), pp. 262–263.

v The Economist Intelligence Unit, Ltd. (2012). *Competing Across Borders: How Cultural and Communication Barriers Affect Business.*

vi Kendra S. Cheruvelil, P. A. Soranno, K. C. Weathers, P. C. Hanson, S. J. Goring, C. T. Filstrup, and E. K. Read (2014). "Creating and Maintaining High-Performing Collaborative Research Teams: The Importance of Diversity and Interpersonal Skills," *Frontiers in Ecology and the Environment*, Vol. 12, no. 1, pp. 31–38. DOI: 10.1890/130001.

vii Julian Schulze and S. Krumm (2017). "The 'Virtual Team Player': A Review and Initial Model of Knowledge, Skills, Abilities, and Other Characteristics for Virtual Collaboration," *Organizational Psychology Review*, Vol. 7, no. 1, pp. 66–95. https://doi.org/10.1177/2041386616675522

viii Jennifer R. Veltsos and G.E. Hynes (2022). *Managerial Communication: Strategies and Applications*, 8th ed. (Thousand Oaks, CA: Sage Publications), p. 3.

ix Towers Watson (2013). *Change and Communication ROI Study Report: How the Fundamentals Have Evolved and the Best Adapt.* Retrieved from towerswatson.com.

x Project Management Institute, Inc. (2013, May). *PMI's Pulse of the Profession In-Depth: The Essential Role of Communication.* Retrieved from www.pmi.org.

Tips for Improving Your Team's Intercultural Communication

1   Reflect on a time you interacted with someone from a different culture. How did you differ in basic communication practices such as eye contact, personal space, direct or indirect communication, or disagreeing?

2   Reflect on something you previously assumed about a team member. Ask yourself how accurate that assumption really was, taking cultural identity into consideration.

3   Ask a team member to elaborate on their idea or perspective on a given issue. Confirm what you have heard in your own words to make sure you understand.

4   Talk to and learn from people who are different from you.

5   Ask another team member how they would approach an upcoming task or how best to communicate a message.

6   Use nonverbal cues such as nodding or smiling to show that you understand and to encourage the speaker to continue.

7   Avoid interrupting – listen attentively until the other person has finished speaking.

8   If you use humor, make sure it will be understood, appreciated, and not cause offense.

Source: Adapted from Patient Centered Outcomes Research Institute (2020). "Intercultural Communication Strategies Tip Sheet," Retrieved April 17, 2022, from www.pcori.org

Conflict Resolution Survey

For each of the 30 statements listed, indicate how frequently you typically behave when you come into conflict with another person. (Rather than responding to these statements generally, you may wish to relate the statements to a particular person or workplace setting.) Use the following scale:

2 = Most of the time
1 = Some of the time
0 = Rarely

_____ 1. I ask for help in resolving the conflict from someone outside our relationship.

_____ 2. I try to stress those things on which we both agree rather than focus on our disagreement.

_____ 3. I suggest we search for a compromise solution acceptable to both of us.

_____ 4. I attempt to bring out all the concerns of the other person.

_____ 5. I am firm in pursuing my goals.

_____ 6. I strive to preserve our relationship.

_____ 7. I seek to split the difference in our positions where possible.

_____ 8. I work toward a solution that meets *both* our needs.

_____ 9. I avoid the discussion of emotionally charged issues.

_____ 10. I try to impose my solution on the other person.

_____ 11. I emphasize whatever similarity I see in our positions.

_____ 12. I try to postpone any discussion until I have had time to think it over.

_____ 13. I propose a middle ground to the other person.

_____ 14. I use whatever power I have to get my wishes.

_____ 15. I attempt to get all our points immediately out in the open.

_____ 16. I give up one point in order to gain another.

_____ 17. I encourage the other person to offer a full explanation of her or his ideas to me.

_____ 18. I try to get the other person to see things my way.
_____ 19. I treat the other person as considerately as possible.
_____ 20. I suggest we think our concerns over individually before we meet in the hope that the anger will cool down.
_____ 21. I press to get my points made.
_____ 22. I support a direct and frank discussion of the problem.
_____ 23. I try to find a fair combination of gains and losses for both of us.
_____ 24. I try not to allow the other person's feelings to become hurt.
_____ 25. I avoid taking positions that would create controversy.
_____ 26. I suggest we each give in on some of our needs to find a solution we can both live with.
_____ 27. I listen carefully in order to understand the other person as well as possible.
_____ 28. I soothe the other person's feelings if emotions are running high.
_____ 29. I assert my position strongly.
_____ 30. I shrink from expressions of hostility.

Score the Conflict Resolution Survey

Fill in the blanks with the same scale scores you entered on the survey. Then total your scores for each conflict resolution approach. Note that the blanks to be filled in do not appear in the same order as the items on the survey.

Scale Score	Item No.	Scale Score	Item No.	Scale Score	Item No.	Scale Score	Item No.	Scale Score	Item No.
	1		2		5		3		4
	9		6		10		7		8
	12		11		14		13		15
	20		19		18		16		17
	25		24		21		23		22
	30		28		29		26		27
Avoiding		Accommo- dating		Forcing		Compro- mising		Collabora- ting	

This is your conflict resolution profile. Note that your score for each approach can range from a low of 0 to a high of 12. The approach with the highest score is your preferred approach to conflict. The second highest is the one you tend to use under pressure.

When to Choose Each Conflict Resolution Approach

Conflict Resolution Approach	Context of Conflict
Avoiding works best when	• There's little chance you'll get your way • The potential damage of addressing the conflict outweighs the benefits of resolution • People need a chance to cool down • Others are in a better position to resolve the conflict • The problem will go away by itself
Accommodating works best when	• Preserving harmony is important • Personal antagonism is the major source of conflict • The issue itself is unsolvable • You care more about the other person than getting your way
Forcing works best when	• Quick, decisive action is needed • A rule has to be enforced • You know you're right • You must protect yourself
Compromising works best when	• Two opponents are equal in power • Temporary settlements on complex issues are needed • Opponents do not share goals • Forcing or collaborating won't work
Collaborating works best when	• Both sets of concerns are too important to be compromised • It is important to work through hard feelings • Commitment to the resolution is important • A permanent solution is desired

Work Plan Template

Purpose: To create a "script" for your improvement effort and to support implementation.

Directions:

1   Using this form as a template, develop a work plan for each goal identified through the needs assessment process. Modify the form as needed to fit your unique context.
2   Distribute copies of each work plan to the members of the collaboration.
3   Keep copies handy to bring to meetings to review and update regularly. You may decide to develop new work plans for new phases of your reform effort.

Goal:

Results/Accomplishments:

Action Steps: What Will Be Done?	Responsibilities: Who Will Do It?	Timeline: By When? (Day/Month)	Resources: A Resources Available B Resources Needed (financial, human, political, and others)	Potential Barriers: A What individuals or organizations might resist? B How?	Communication Plan: Who is involved? What methods? How often?
Step 1:			A.	A.	
			B.	B.	
Step 2:			A.	A.	
			B.	B.	
Step 3:			A.	A.	
			B.	B.	
Step 4:			A.	A.	
			B.	B.	
Step 5:			A.	A.	
			B.	B.	

Evidence of Success (How will you know that you are making progress? What are your benchmarks?)

Evaluation Process (How will you determine that your goal has been reached? What are your measures?)

Bibliography

Abu-Arquoub, I. A., and F. A. Alserhan (2019). "Non-Verbal Barriers to Effective Intercultural Communication," *Utopía Y Praxis Latinoamericana*, vol. 24, no. 5, pp. 307–316.

American Management Association (2019, April 8). "The Latest on Workplace Monitoring and Surveillance." Retrieved from https://www.amanet.org/articles/the-latest-on-workplace-monitoring-and-surveillance

Ballentine, C., and A. McNeely (2022, April 1). "Employees Are Returning to the Office, Just to Sit on Zoom Calls," *Bloomberg Wealth*. Retrieved from https://www.bloomberg.com/news/articles/2022-04-01/employees-are-returning-to-office-post-covid-just-to-sit-on-zoom-calls

Becker, B. E., and R. J. Klimoski (1989). "A Field Study of the Relationship Between the Organizational Feedback Environment and Performance," *Personnel Psychology*, vol. 42, no. 3, pp. 343–358.

Beebe, S. A., T. P. Mottet, and K. D. Roach (2012). *Training and Development: Communicating for Success*, 2nd ed. (New York: Pearson).

Bennett, L. M., and H. Gadlin (2012). "Collaboration and Team Science: From Theory to Practice," *Journal of Investigative Medicine*, vol. 60, no. 5, pp. 768–775. 10.231/JIM.0b013e318250871d2019

Bennett, M. J. (1986). "A Developmental Approach to Training for Intercultural Sensitivity," *International Journal of Intercultural Relations*, vol. 10, pp. 179–196.

Bolchover, D. (2012). "Competing Across Borders: How Cultural and Communication Barriers Affect Business." *The Economist Intelligence Unit Ltd. Report*, p. 11.

Bradberry, T., and J. Greaves (2009). *Emotional Intelligence 2.0. San Diego, CA:* (Talent Smart).

Breer, A. (2022, May 19). "Inside the Plans for the NFL's First Diversity Networking Event," *Sports Illustrated*. Retrieved from https://www.si.com/nfl/2022/05/19/nfl-diversity-networking-event-plans-spring-meeting

Bregenzer, A., B. Milfelner, S. Šarotar Žižek, and P. Jiménez (2020). "Health-Promoting Leadership And Leaders' Listening Skills Have an Impact on the Employees' Job Satisfaction and Turnover Intention," *International Journal of Business Communication*, 2329488420963700. https://doi.org/10.1177/2329488420963700

Bryant, A. (2014, August 3). "See Yourself as Others See You: Interview with Sharon Sloane." *The New York Times*, p. 2.

Carney, D. R. (2021, February). "Ten Things Every Manager Should Know about Nonverbal Behavior," *California Management Review*, vol. 63, no. 2, pp. 5–22.

Carroll, A. B. (2006, July 29). "Trust Is the Key When Rating Great Workplaces." Retrieved from http://onlineathens.com/stories/073006/business_20060730047. shtml, p. 1.

Cederblom, D. (1992). "The Performance Appraisal Interview: A Review, Implications, and Suggestions," in Kevin L. Hutchinson (ed.), *Readings in Organizational Communication*, (Dubuque, IA: Wm. C. Brown), pp. 310–321.

Cheruvelil, K. S., P. A. Soranno, K. C. Weathers, P. C. Hanson, S. J. Goring, C. T. Filstrup, and E. K. Read (2014). "Creating and Maintaining High-Performing Collaborative Research Teams: The Importance of Diversity and Interpersonal Skills." *Frontiers in Ecology and the Environment*, vol. 12, no. 1, pp. 31–38. 10.1890/130001

Colvin, G. (1999, July 19). "Outperforming the S&P 500: Companies that Pursue Diversity Outperform the S&P 500. Coincidence?" *Fortune*, vol. 140, no. 2.

Conrad, R. (2019). *Culture Hacks: Deciphering Differences in American, Chinese, and Japanese Thinking* (Austin, Texas: Lioncrest Publishing), p. 14.

Contreras, A., A. Dey, and C. Hill (2020). "'Tone at the Top' and the Communication of Corporate Values: Lost in Translation?," *Seattle University Law Review*, vol. 43, no. 2, pp. 497–523.

Culbert, S. A. (2010). *Get Rid of the Performance Review! How Companies Can Stop Intimidating, Start Managing, and Focus on What Really Matters* (New York, NY: Hachette Book Group).

DeSmet, A., B. Dowling, M. Mugayar-Baldocchi, and B. Schanninger (2021). "'Great Attrition' or 'Great Attraction'? The Choice Is Yours," *McKinsey Quarterly*. Retrieved from https://www.mckinsey.com/business-functions/people-and-organizational-performance/our-insights/great-attrition-or-great-attraction-the-choice-is-yours

Donohue, W. A., M. E. Diez, and R. B. Stahl (1983). "New Directions in Negotiations Research," in R. N. Bostrom (ed.), *Communication Yearbook 7* (Thousand Oaks, CA: SAGE Publications), pp. 249–279.

Downs, T. M. (1990). "Predictions of Communication Satisfaction During Performance Appraisal Interviews," *Management Communication Quarterly*, vol. 3, no. 13, pp. 334–354.

Dugan, B. (1988). "Effects of Assessor Training on Information Use," *Journal of Applied Psychology*, vol. 73, pp. 743–748.

Edelman Trust Barometer (2012). Executive summary. Retrieved from http://www.scribd.com/doc/79026497/2012-Edelman-Trust-Barometer-Executive-Summary.

Elmuti, D., and H. H. Davis (2006). "Not Worth the Bad Will," *Industrial Management*, vol. 48, no. 6, pp. 26–30.

Erbert, L. A. (2014). "Antagonistic and Non-Antagonistic Dialectical Contradictions in Organizational Conflict," *International Journal of Business Communication*, vol. 51, no. 2, pp. 138–158.

Fluker, D. (2021, May 8). "12 Companies Ramping Up Their Diversity & Inclusion Efforts - and How You Can Too," *Glassdoor for Employers*. Retrieved from https://www.glassdoor.com/employers/blog/inspiration-for-ramping-up-diversity-inclusion-efforts/

Forbes, M. (2013, November 1). "7 Career Lessons from Billionaire Abigail Johnson," *Forbes*. Retrieved from https://www.forbes.com/sites/moiraforbes/2013/11/01/seven-career-lessons-from-billionaire-abigail-johnson/?sh=26d83d8276a1

Gagne, R. (n.d.). *Nine Events of Instruction*. Retrieved from http://www.instructionaldesign.org/theories/conditions-learning.html

Gammage, J. (2006, January 29). "Good Liars May be Wired Differently," *Houston Chronicle*, p. 2D.

Garner, J. L. (2011). "How Award-Winning Professors in Higher Education Use Merrill's First Principles of Instruction," *International Journal of Instructional Technology and Distance Learning*, vol. 8, no. 5, pp. 3–16.

Gelles, D. (2022, April 3). "No Longer Running but Still in the Race," *The New York Times*, p. 4.

Gibb, J. R. (1961, September). "Defensive Communication," *Journal of Communication*, pp. 141–148. 10.1111/j.1460-2466.1961.tb00344.x

Gladwell, M. (2008). *Outliers: The Story of Success* (New York: Little, Brown and Company).

Goldberg, E. (2022, March 10). "A Two-Year, 50-Million-Person Experiment in Changing How We Work," *The New York Times*. Retrieved from https://www.nytimes.com/2022/03/10/business/remote-work-office-life.html

Goleman, D. (1995). *Emotional Intelligence* (New York, NY: Bantam Publishing Co.).

Gosling, S. (2008). *Snoop: What Your Stuff Says About You* (London, UK: Profile Books).

Grant, A. (2013). *Give and Take: A Revolutionary Approach to Success* (New York, NY: Viking Press).

Grant, A., and S. Sandberg (2014, December 7). "Women at Work: When Talking about Bias Backfires." *The New York Times*, P. 3SR.

Gudykunst, W. B. (1998). *Bridging Differences: Effective Intergroup Communication*, 3rd ed. (Thousand Oaks, CA: SAGE Publishing).

Hamilton, C. (2013). *Communicating for Results: A Guide for Business and the Professions*, 10th ed. (New York: Cengage).

Hargie, O., D. Tourish, and N. Wilson (2001). "Communication Audits and the Effects of Increased Information: A Follow-Up Study," *Journal of Business Communication*, vol. 39, no. 4, pp. 414–436.

Hart Research Associates (2013). *It Takes More than a Major: Employer Priorities for College Learning and Student Success* (Washington, DC: Association of American Colleges and Universities).

Hoffman, L. R., E. Harburg, and N. R. F. Meier (1962). "Differences and Disagreements as Factors in Creative Problem-Solving," *Journal of Abnormal and Social Psychology*, vol. 64, no. 2, pp. 206–224.

Hoffower, H. (2022, May 8). "Meet the Typical Gen Z Worker, Who Is Quitting Their Job for a Better One but Probably Regretting it Later," *Business Insider*. Retrieved from https://www.businessinsider.com/what-gen-z-wants-workplace-expecations-salary-benefits-perks-2022-5

Hofstede, G. (1980, Summer). "Motivation, Leadership and Organization: Do American Theories Apply Abroad?" *Organizational Dynamics*, pp. 42–63.

Hofstede, G. and Associates (1998). *Masculinity and Femininity: The Taboo Dimension of National Cultures* (Thousand Oaks, CA: SAGE Publishing), p. 37.

HR Research Institute (2018). "The State of Employee Engagement in 2018: Leverage Leadership and Culture to Maximize Engagement." Retrieved from https://www.hr.com/en/resources/free_research_white_papers/the-state-of-employee-engagement-in-2018-mar2018_jeqfvgoq.html

Hughes, L. (2004, January–February). "Do's and Don'ts of Effective Team Leadership," *WIB, Magazine of the American Business Women's Association*, p. 10.

Hurst, A. (2014, April 20). "Being 'Good' Isn't the Only Way to Go." *Houston Chronicle*. p. B2.

"Inaugural NFL Coach and Front Office Accelerator Program" (2022, May 19). Retrieved from https://www.nfl.com/news/inaugural-nfl-coach-and-front-office-accelerator-program-slated-for-spring-league

Institute for the Future (2011). "Future Work Skills 2020." *Institute for the Future for the University of Phoenix Research Institute*. Retrieved from www.iftf.org

Jayne, M. E. A., and R. Dipboye (2004, Winter). "Leveraging Diversity to Improve Business Performance: Research Findings and Recommendations for Organizations." *Human Resource Management*, vol. 43, no. 4, pp. 409–424.

Kadazdaj, B., and V. Hamiti (2020). "Nonverbal Communication in German-Albanian Cultural Contrast." *Sakarya University Journal of Education*, vol. 10, no. 1, pp. 187–201. 10.19126/suje.689503

Kameda, N. (2014). "Japanese Business Discourse of Oneness: A Personal Perspective." *International Journal of Business Communication*, vol. 51, no. 1, pp. 93–113.

Kelly, J. (2021, May 21). "Survey Asks Employees at Top U.S. Companies if They'd Give Up $30,000 to WFH: The Answer May Surprise You." *Forbes*. Retrieved from https://www.forbes.com/sites/jackkelly/2021/05/21/survey-asks-employees-at-top-us-companies-if-theyd-give-up-30000-to-work-from-home-the-answers-may-surprise-you/?sh=55749769330f

Kirkpatrick, A. (2009). *World Englishes: Implications for International Communication and English Language Teaching* (Cambridge, England: Cambridge University Press).

Kirkpatrick, D., and J. D. Kirkpatrick (2007). *Implementing the Four Levels* (Berrett-Koehler Publishers).

Knapp, M. L., and M. S. McGlone (2016). *Lying + Deception in Human Interaction*, 2nd ed. (Dubuque, IA: Kendall Hunt).

Kochan, T., K. Bezrukova, R. Ely, S. Jackson, A. Joshi, K. Jehn, et al. (2003). "The Effects of Diversity on Business Performance: Report of the Diversity Research Network." *Human Resource Management*, vol. 42, pp. 3–21.

Kolb, D., and R. Fry (1975). "Toward an Applied Theory of Experiential Learning," in C. Cooper (ed.), *Theories of Group Process* (London: John Wiley & Sons).

Krawcheck, S. (2014, March 24). "Diversify Corporate America," *Time*, pp. 36–37.

"Leadership in Diversity and Inclusion" (2014, November 9). *New York Times Magazine*, pp. 54–58.

Lewis, P. V. (1987). *Organizational Communication: The Essence of Effective Management*, 3rd ed. (New York: Wiley & Sons).

Lohr, S. (2014, June 21). "Unblinking Eyes Track Employees: Workplace Surveillance Sees Good and Bad," *The New York Times*. Retrieved from http://www.nytimes.com/2014/06/22/technology/workplace-surveillance-sees-good-and-bad.html?_r=0

Maier, R. F. (1958). *The Appraisal Interview: Objectives and Skills* (New York: John Wiley & Sons).

MassMutual (2021). "Our commitment to diversity, equity, and inclusion." Retrieved from https://www.massmutual.com/sustainability/diversity-equity-and-inclusion/unity-messaging

MassMutual (2021). "Sustainability Report," p. 18. Retrieved from https://www.massmutual.com/global/media/shared/doc/sustainability/2021sustainabilityreport.pdf#page=23

McClintock, C. J., and R. G. Hunt (1975). "Nonverbal Indicators of Affect and Deception in Interview Situations," *Journal of Applied Psychology*, vol. 5, no. 3, p. 420.

McGregor, D. (1960). *The Human Side of Enterprise* (New York: McGraw-Hill).

McWhorter, J. (2022, May 15). "'I Feel Like' There's no Problem Here." *The New York Times*, p. SR9.

McWorthy, L., and D. D. Henningsen (2014). "Looking at Favorable and Unfavorable Superior-Subordinate Relationships through Dominance and Affiliation Lenses," *International Journal of Business Communication*, vol. 51, no. 2, pp. 123–137.

Merrill, M. D. (2002). "First Principles of Instruction," *Educational Technology Research and Development*, vol. 50, no. 3, pp. 43–59.

Meyer, E. (2015). *The Culture Map: Breaking Through the Invisible Boundaries of Global Business* (New York: Public Affairs), pp. 219–242.

Mirivel, J. C. (2014). *The Art of Positive Communication: Theory and Practice* (New York: Peter Lang Publishing).

Mirivel, J. C., R. Fuller, A. Young, and K. Christman (2022, January 30). "Integrating Positive Communication Principles and Practices in Business Communication Courses," *The Western Association for Business Communication Bulletin*. Retrieved from https://abcwest.org/2022/01/30/integrating-positive-communication-principles-and-practices-in-business-communication-courses/

Mishra, K., L. Boynton, and A. Mishra (2014). "Driving Employee Engagement: The Expanded Role of Internal Communications," *International Journal of Business Communication*, vol. 51, no. 2, p. 191.

Moore, A. D. (2000). "Employee Monitoring and Computer Technology: Evaluative Surveillance v. Privacy," *Business Ethics Quarterly*, vol. 10, no. 3, pp. 697–709.

Morgan Stanley (2021, November 8). "A Single Mom Returns to Work." Retrieved from https://www.morganstanley.com/articles/return-to-work-single-mom-erica-bowman

Morris, M., and K. Leung (2000). "Justice for All? Progress in Research on Cultural Variation in the Psychology of Distributive and Procedural Justice," *Applied Psychology: An International Review*, vol. 49, no. 1, pp. 100–132.

Mullin, M. (2022, April 22). "Kyle Neptune Ready to Embrace 'Monumental Task'," *The Philadelphia Inquirer*. Retrieved from https://www.inquirer.com/college-sports/villanova/live/villanova-jay-wright-retirement-kyle-neptune-fordham-20220422.html

Munter, M. (2012). *Guide to Managerial Communication: Effective Business Writing and Speaking*, 9th ed. (New York: Prentice Hall).

Murphy, M. (2021). "Why New Hires Fail," *Leadership IQ* Blog. Retrieved from https://www.leadershipiq.com/blogs/leadershipiq/35354241-why-new-hires-fail-emotional-intelligence-vs-skills

Nadkarni, A., N. C. Levy-Carrick, D. S. Kroll, D. Gitlin, and D. Silbersweig (2021). "Communication and Transparency as a Means to Strengthening Workplace Culture During COVID-19," *NAM Perspectives, National Academy of Medicine*, Washington, DC. Retrieved from 10.31478/202103a

Nisbett, R. (2004). *The Geography of Thought: How Asians and Westerners Think Differently ... and Why* (Glencoe, IL: Free Press).

"Oakwood Worldwide Honored by Training Magazine for Fifth Consecutive Year: Training also Presents Oakwood with Best Practice Award" (2011, February 25). *Marketwire*. Retrieved from http://www.live-pr.com/en/oakwood-worldwide-honored-by-training-magazine-r1048761409.htm

Patient-Centered Outcomes Research Institute (2020). "Building Effective Multi-Stakeholder Research Teams." Retrieved from https://research-teams.pcori.org/stakeholders#Practicing%20Effective%20Team%20Communication

Patient-Centered Outcomes Research Institute (2021). "Negotiating Personal Conflict Tip Sheet." Retrieved from www.pcori.org

Peters, J. (2019). *Employee Engagement: Creating High Positive Energy at Work* (Randburg, South Africa: KR Publishing).

Porath, C. (2016). *Mastering Civility: A Manifesto for the Workplace* (New York: Grand Central Publishing).

Project Management Institute, Inc. (2013, May). "The High Cost of Low Performance: The Essential Role of Communications," *Pulse of the Profession In-depth Report*. Retrieved from www.pmi.org

Prudential Financial, Inc. Proxy Statement (2022). Retrieved from https://www.prudential.com/links/about/board-of-directors

Putnam, L., and S. Wilson (1988). "Argumentation and Bargaining Strategies as Discriminators of Integrative and Distributive Outcomes," in A. Rahim (ed.), *Managing Conflict: An Interdisciplinary Approach* (New York: Praeger Publishers).

Quirk, B. (2008). *Making the Connections: Using Internal Communication to Turn Strategy into Action* (Burlington, VT: Gower).

Rainie, L., and M. Duggan (2016, January 14). "Privacy and Information Sharing," *Pew Research Center*. Retrieved from http://www.pewinternet.org/2016/01/14/privacy-and-information-sharing

Ramirez-Esparza, N., S. D. Gosling, V. Benet-Martinez, J. P. Potter, and J. W. Pennebaker (2006). "Do Bilinguals Have Two Personalities? A Special Case of Cultural Frame Switching," *Journal of Research in Personality*, vol. 40, pp. 99–120.

Rasberry, R. (2013, March 15). "A Study of How Fortune 100 Companies Communicate Ethics, Governance, Corporate Responsibility, Sustainability, and Human Rights," Paper presented at the Association for Business Communication-Southwestern U.S. Annual Conference, Albuquerque, NM.

Robison, J. (2012, January 5). "Boosting Engagement at Stryker," *Gallup Management Journal*. Retrieved from http://gmj.gallup.com/content/150956/Boosting-Engagement-Stryker.aspx.

Ross, H. J. (2014, August 3). "An Appeal to Our Inner Judge," *The New York Times*, p. D3.

Rothfelder, J. (2014). *Driving Honda: Inside the World's Most Innovative Car Company* (New York: Portfolio/Penguin).

Russ, G. S., R.L. Daft, and R.H. Lengel (1990, November). "Media Selection and Managerial Characteristics in Organizational Communications," *Management Communication Quarterly*, vol. 4, no. 2, pp. 151–175.

Ryback, D. (2012). *Putting Emotional Intelligence to Work* (New York: Routledge).

Sarnoff, N. (2014, June 13). "Younger Workers Crave 'Sense of Place' on the Job." *Houston Chronicle*, p. D1.

Schmidt, W. V., R. N. Conaway, S. S. Easton, and W. J. Wardrope (2007). *Communicating Globally: Intercultural Communication and International Business* (Thousand Oaks, CA: SAGE Publications).

Schooley, S. (2022, July 7). "How to be a Good Manager." *Business News Daily*. Retrieved from https://www.businessnewsdaily.com/6129-good-manager-skills.html

Schreiber-Shearer, N. (2022, April 11). "3 Companies Showcasing Successful Mentorship Programs." Retrieved from https://gloat.com/blog/successful-mentorship-programs/

Schroeder, J., and J.L. Risen (2014, July 28). "Befriending the Enemy: Outgroup Friendship Longitudinally Predicts Intergroup Attitudes in a Coexistence Program for Israelis and Palestinians." *Group Processes and Intergroup Relations Journal.* 10.1177/ 1368430214542257

Schulze, J., and S. Krumm (2017). "The 'Virtual Team Player': A Review and Initial Model of Knowledge, Skills, Abilities, and Other Characteristics for Virtual Collaboration," *Organizational Psychology Review*, vol. 7, no. 1, pp. 66–95. 10.1177/ 2041386616675522

Schwartz, T., and C. Porath (2014, June 1). "Why You Hate Work," *New York Times*, p. 1SR.

Shafiq, M., M. Zia-ur-Rehman, and M. Rashid (2013). "Impact of Compensation, Training and Development and Supervisory Support on Organizational Commitment," *Compensation and Benefits Review*, vol. 45, no. 5, pp. 278–285.

Shirley, D. (1998). *Managing Martians: The Extraordinary Story of a Woman's Lifelong Quest to Get to Mars -- and of the Team Behind the Space Robot That Captured the Imagination of the World* (New York: Broadway Books).

Sicorello, M., J. Stevanov, H. Ashida, and H. Hecht (2019). "Effect of Gaze on Personal Space: A Japanese–German Cross-Cultural Study," *Journal of Cross-Cultural Psychology*, vol. 50, no. 1, pp. 8–21. 10.1177/0022022118798513

Sigband, N., and A. Bell (1986). *Communicating for Management and Business*, 4th ed. (Glenview, IL: Scott Foresman).

Sigmar, L. S., G. E. Hynes, and K. L. Hill (2012). "Strategies for Teaching Social and Emotional Intelligence in Business Communication," *Business Communication Quarterly*, vol. 75, no. 3, pp. 301–317.

Sixel, I. M. (2013, May 16). "Permission to Speak Freely to the Boss," *Houston Chronicle*, p. D1.

Sotomayor, S. (2014). *My Beloved World* (New York: Vintage Book).

Stipleman, B. A., E. Rice, A.L. Vogel, and K.L. Hall (2019). "Comprehensive Collaboration Plans: Practical Considerations Spanning Across Individual Collaborators to Institutional Supports," in K. L. Hall, A. L. Vogel, & R. T. Croyle (eds.), *Strategies for Team Science Success* (Springer), pp. 587–611. 10.1007/978-3-030-20992-6_45

Subramanian, S. (2021, March 11). "A New Era of Workplace Inclusion: Moving from Retrofit to Redesign," *Future Forum* blog. Retrieved from https://futureforum.com/ 2021/03/11/dismantling-the-office-moving-from-retrofit-to-redesign/

Tannen, D. (2007). *You Just Don't Understand: Women and Men in Conversation* (New York: William Morrow).

Taylor, M. (2022, March 14). "How to Communicate Well with People From Other Cultures." *wikiHow* blog. Retrieved from https://www.wikihow.com/Communicate-Well-With-People-from-Other-Cultures

The Ladders Quarterly Remote Work Report (2022). Retrieved from https://www.theladders. com/wp-content/uploads/Ladders-Inc-Q1-2022-Quarterly-Work-Report.pdf

"The Present (and Future) of Business Communications" (July 25, 2005). *Accounting Web*. Retrieved from http://www.accountingweb.com

Thomas, G. F. (2020, November). "Perspective: Managing Virtual Team Conflict," *The Western ABC Bulletin*, vol. 2, no. 2. Association for Business Communication. Retrieved from https://abcwest.org

Toossi, M. (2013, December). "Labor Force Projections to 2022," *Monthly Labor Review*. Retrieved from www.bls.gov/EMP

Towers Watson (2013). *Change and Communication ROI Study – The 10th Anniversary Report*. Retrieved from www.towerswatson.com

U.S. Bureau of Labor Statistics (2021, November). "Labor Force Characteristics by Race and Ethnicity, 2020." *BLS Reports*. Retrieved from https://www.bls.gov/opub/reports/race-and-ethnicity/2020/home.htm

Valukas, A. R. (2014). "Report to Board of Directors of General Motors Company Regarding Ignition Switch Recalls," *Detroit: Jenner & Block*. Retrieved from http://www.Scribd.com/doc/228310223/GM-s-Valukas-Switch-Recall-Report, p. 250.

Veltsos, J. R., and G. E. Hynes (2022). *Managerial Communication: Strategies and Applications*, 8th ed. (Thousand Oaks, CA: SAGE Publications).

Vickery, H. B. (1984, January). "Tapping into the Employee Grapevine," *Association Management*, pp. 59–64.

Waltman, J. L. (1983, June). "Nonverbal Interrogation: Some Applications," *Journal of Police Science and Administration*, vol. 11, no. 2, p. 167.

Wen, H. J., D. Schwieger, and P. Gershuny (2007). "Internet Usage Monitoring in the Workplace: Its Legal Challenges and Implementation Strategies," *Information Systems Management*, vol. 24, no. 2, pp. 185–196.

Whalen, J. (2022, March). "A Scientific Explanation for the Degree of Misunderstanding When Communicating," *Association for Business Communication Newsletter*. Retrieved from www.businesscommunication.org.

Wood, J. T. (2013). *Gendered Lives: Communication, Gender, and Culture*, 10th ed. (Boston: Wadsworth).

Yang, M., and S. L. Watson (2021). "Attitudinal Influences on Transfer of Training: A Systematic Literature Review," *Performance Improvement Quarterly*, vol. 34, Issue 4, pp. 327–365. 10.1002/piq

Youssef, M., K. Mokni, and A. N. Ajmi (2021). "Dynamic Connectedness Between Stock Markets in the Presence of the COVID-19 Pandemic: Does Economic Policy Uncertainty Matter?" *Financial Innovation*, vol. 7, Issue 1, pp. 1–27. 10.1186/s40854-021-00227-3.

Zolin, G. F. T. R., and J. L. Hartman (2009). "The Central Role of Communication in Developing Trust and Its Effect on Employee Involvement," *Journal of Business Communication*, vol. 46, no. 3, pp. 287–310.

Index

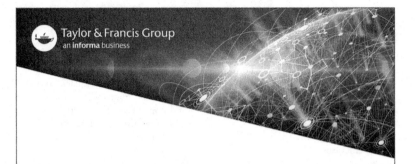

Printed in the United States
by Baker & Taylor Publisher Services